The church should have copies of Dr Trentham's books on sale in the narthex.

B. R.

# Studies in Timothy

*Studies in*

# TIMOTHY

Charles A. Trentham

*Convention Press*

NASHVILLE                    TENNESSEE

© 1959 • CONVENTION PRESS
Nashville, Tennessee

511-00217

Library of Congress Catalog Card Number: 59-9965

*Printed in the United States of America*

395. AL 59 R.R.D.

*To Helen*

WHO MIGHT HAVE WRITTEN THIS BOOK

IF SHE HAD HAD A WIFE

# About the Author

CHARLES ARTHUR TRENTHAM was born in Jefferson City, Tennessee, July 2, 1919, and later moved with his parents to Knoxville, Tennessee. He attended Mars Hill Junior College and received the B.A. degree from Carson-Newman College. While there he served as president of the Philomathean Society and as pastor of the Piedmont, Benton, and New Market Baptist churches. He received the Th.M. and Th.D. degrees from Southwestern Baptist Theological Seminary, where he graduated with honors and was speaker for his class. During his student days at the seminary he served as pastor of the Sycamore Heights Baptist Church. He has taught in the Department of Religion, Baylor University, and has served at Southwestern as student assistant to Dr. W. T. Conner and later as professor in the Systematic Theology Department for seven years. Dr. Trentham received the Ph.D. degree from the University of Edinburgh, Scotland.

Since 1953 he has been pastor of the First Baptist Church of Knoxville, Tennessee, and for the past several years has served as dean of the School of Religion of the University of Tennessee. He is a trustee of Carson-Newman College and of the East Tennessee Baptist Hospital, and has served on the Sunday School Board of the Southern Baptist Convention and on the Survey Committee of the Tennessee Baptist Convention. His published writings include Adult and Young People's Sunday school lessons; Young People's Training

Union programs; contributions to *Open Windows, The Baptist Student* magazine, *The Baptist Training Union Magazine,* and the book *Christian Faith in Action* compiled by Foy Valentine.

Dr. Trentham recently preached on the Columbia Broadcasting System's "Church of the Air" and in 1958 delivered the Theological Lectures at the Golden Gate Baptist Theological Seminary in Berkeley, California. He is a Rotarian.

Dr. Trentham married Helen King Berry of Knoxville, Tennessee. They have two sons, David Earl, age 13, and Robert Lee, age 11.

# Contents

Church Study Course for Teaching and Training...... xi

Requirements for Credit in Class or Home Study...... xiii

Some Projected Audio-Visual Materials.............. xv

Introduction ..................................... 1

## PART ONE—1 TIMOTHY

1. TIMOTHY RECEIVES HIS COMMISSION................ 9
2. PROPER PROCEDURES FOR PUBLIC WORSHIP............ 27
3. QUALIFICATIONS FOR PASTORS AND DEACONS......... 37
4. CHARACTERISTICS OF A GOOD MINISTER............. 49
5. HOW VARIOUS CHURCH GROUPS SHOULD BE TREATED.... 61
6. FINAL CALL TO FAITHFULNESS.................... 77

## PART TWO—2 TIMOTHY

7. GRATITUDE FOR TIMOTHY'S MINISTRY............... 87
8. THE DEATH THAT BRINGS LIFE.....................103
9. THE PASTOR'S SOLEMN CHARGE....................117
10. THE MARTYR'S CROWN...........................135

Questions for Review and Examination...............143

# Church Study Course for Teaching and Training

THE CHURCH STUDY COURSE for Teaching and Training began October 1, 1959. It is a merger of three courses previously promoted by the Baptist Sunday School Board—the Sunday School Training Course, the Graded Training Union Study Course, and the Church Music Training Course.

The course is fully graded. The system of awards provides a series of five diplomas of twenty books each for Adults or Young People, one diploma of ten books for Young People, two diplomas of five books each for Intermediates, and two diplomas of five books each for Juniors. All book awards earned previously in the Sunday School Training Course, the Graded Training Union Study Course, and the Church Music Training Course may be transferred to the new course.

The course is comprehensive, with books grouped into nineteen categories. The purpose of the course is to (1) help Christians to grow in knowledge and conviction; (2) help them grow toward maturity in Christian character and competence for service; (3) encourage them to participate worthily as workers in their churches, and (4) develop leaders for all phases of church life and work.

The Church Study Course for Teaching and Training is promoted by the Baptist Sunday School Board, 127 Ninth Avenue, North, Nashville, Tennessee, through its Sunday School, Training Union, Church Music, and Church Administration departments, and by these same departments in the states affiliated with the Southern Baptist Convention. A complete description of the course and the system of awards may be found in the *Church Study Course for Teaching and Training* catalog which may be obtained without charge from any one of these departments.

A record of all awards earned should be maintained in each church. A person should be designated by the church to keep the files. Forms for such records may be ordered from any Baptist Book Store.

# Requirements for Credit in Class or Home Study

IF CREDIT IS DESIRED for the study of this book in a class or by home study the following requirements must be met:

## I. IN CLASSWORK

1. The class must meet a minimum of seven and one-half clock hours. The required time does not include assembly periods. Ten class periods of forty-five minutes each are recommended. (If laboratory or clinical work is desired in specialized or technical courses, this requirement may be met by six clock hours of classwork and three clock hours of supervised laboratory or clinical work.)

2. A class member who attends all class sessions and completes the reading of the book within a week following the class session will not be required to do any written work.

3. A class member who is absent from one or more sessions must answer the questions on all chapters he misses. In such a case, he must turn in his paper within a week and must certify that the book has been read.

4. The teacher should request an award for himself. A person who teaches a book in sections B, C, or D of any category or conducts an approved unit of instruction for Nursery, Beginner, or Primary children will be granted an award in category 11, Special Studies, which will count as an elective on his own diploma. He should specify in his request the name of the book taught, or the unit conducted for Nursery, Beginners, or Primaries.

5. The teacher should complete the Request for Book Award—Class Study (Form 150) and forward it within two weeks after the completion of the class to the Church Study Course Awards Office, 127 Ninth Avenue, North, Nashville 3, Tennessee.

## II. IN HOME STUDY

1. A person who does not attend any class session may receive credit by answering all questions for written work as indicated in the book. When a person turns in his paper on home study, he must certify that he has read the book.

2. Students may find profit in studying the text together, but individual papers are required. Carbon copies or duplicates in any form cannot be accepted.

3. Home study work papers may be graded by the pastor or a person designated by him, or they may be sent to the Church Study Course Awards Office for grading. The form Request for Book Award—Home Study (Form 151) must be used in requesting awards. It should be mailed to Church Study Course Awards Office, 127 Ninth Avenue, North, Nashville 3, Tennessee.

## III. CREDIT FOR THIS BOOK

This book is in category 2, section A.

# Some Projected Audio-Visual Materials

## FOR USE IN TEACHING THIS BOOK

IF THERE IS MORE material listed than it will be practical for you to use, select the frames of the filmstrips and portions of motion pictures that contribute most directly to the chapters of the book and that most nearly meet the needs of the group you are teaching.

*Studies in Timothy*, a color filmstrip, was prepared especially for use in teaching this book. It is recommended for use as introduction to and/or summary of the book.

In addition, the following background materials may be used:

### FILMSTRIPS (each with manual)

*Men of Good Report* (33 frames, color)
*Chosen Vessels* (39 frames, color)
*This They Believed* (42 frames, color)
*If God Be for Us* (43 frames, color)
*Crown of Righteousness* (38 frames, color)
*A Lost Jailer* (39 frames, color)

### MOTION PICTURES

*What Must I Do to Be Saved* (18 min., sound)
*Triumphant* (17 min., sound)

### SLIDES

N 244 *Paul Dictating an Epistle*
Ha 817 *Timothy and His Mother*

# INTRODUCTION

ALL OF THE PASTORAL EPISTLES (1 Timothy, 2 Timothy, Titus) name the apostle Paul as their author. In addition to this fact, there is a great unbroken tradition which inisists that Paul wrote them. We cannot honestly overlook, however, the fact that a considerable number of scholars have contested this claim.

Such scholars have found many words in the vocabulary of the pastoral epistles which do not appear in the known writings of Paul (see 1 Tim. 1:12; 2:2; 6:11; 2 Tim. 2:22). Moreover, the pastorals describe visits to Ephesus (1 Tim. 1:3), to Miletus (2 Tim. 4:20), to Troas (2 Tim. 4:13), a mission to Crete, and possibly missions in Gaul and Dalmatia (2 Tim. 4:10), which are difficult to harmonize with the accounts of Paul's journeys in Acts. Furthermore, some competent scholars have felt that the details of church organization described in the epistle to Timothy did not come into being until after the death of Paul.

We cannot deal adequately with these objections to the Pauline authorship within this brief treatment. So far as the vocabulary is concerned, we may well believe that the subject matter of the pastorals is so different from that of the previous epistles that Paul would necessarily be using some words he had not previously employed. Moreover, Paul was an old man when he wrote these epistles and his vocabulary may well have taken on new and larger meaning in the intervening years.

1

With respect to the difficulty in harmonizing the pastoral accounts of Paul's journeys with those in Acts, we may say that it is very likely that Paul was released from the Roman imprisonment described in Acts, and thus was permitted to return to the East for a visit in Ephesus, Troas, Miletus, Corinth, Crete, and elsewhere. During this period he wrote 1 Timothy and Titus. We may also believe that he was later arrested, and that during his second imprisonment he wrote 2 Timothy.

Many feel that it is incredible that Paul should have been put to death on such meager charges as those preferred at his first arrest (Acts 25:27). It is felt that upon a second arrest far more specific and damaging charges were made against him.

It is quite evident that Paul anticipated release from his first imprisonment, for he wrote most hopefully about a favorable outcome of his trial both to Philemon (v. 22) and to the Philippians 2:19–24). He even arranged to visit them again.

There is, however, an honest difficulty at this point. Paul told the elders of Ephesus that they should see his face no more (Acts 20:25). Howbeit, the pastorals affirm that he did see their faces again. This fact should not, however, be a determining factor in deciding the authorship of the pastoral epistles. It may indicate simply that there was an interruption of Paul's plans after his release from prison, which made it necessary for him to alter his original intention.

With respect to the claim that the church of the first century was not as highly organized as the one described by the author of the pastorals, it should be said that the church grew and developed most rapidly in its early years.

Dr. Newport J. D. White declared concerning the development of the church:

> In the first century a year thus wrought what it now takes a generation to effect. . . . It was while the church was rapidly

taking shape that St. Paul came into it; and, if we may judge from extant evidence, he quickly became the most powerful constructive force in it.[1]

Let it be said in closing the discussion as to the authorship of the pastoral epistles that the preponderance of evidence seems to be with the traditional point of view which believes that Paul, the aged apostle, was in these letters writing to his son in the ministry, Timothy.

## I. The Recipient of These Letters

It is quite natural to accept the view that the first two pastoral epistles were addressed to Timothy. Fortunately, we know as much about Timothy as about any of Paul's companions. He was converted under Paul's ministry and was called Paul's beloved and faithful son in the Lord (I Cor. 4:17). In 1 Timothy 1:2 he is called "Timothy, my true child in faith" (ASV).

Timothy lived, probably, at Lystra, which was evangelized by Paul during his first missionary journey (Acts 14:6–22; 16:1). He was chosen in the early part of Paul's apostolic career to be his companion. Timothy's steadfast friendship carried through to the end of the great apostle's life.

Twice we are told in the Scriptures that Timothy's father was a Greek (Acts 16:1–3). His mother, Eunice, was a Jewess. His devout grandmother was named Lois (2 Tim. 1:5). We assume that Eunice was converted on Paul's first missionary journey to Derbe and Lystra, because when he returned later to these cities she is mentioned as a Jewess who believed (Acts 16:1). We are told how deeply impressed Paul was with Timothy, seeing his "unfeigned faith" and that from a child he had been taught the sacred Scriptures of the Old Testament (2 Tim. 3:15). His strong Christian character combined with such training to equip him most admirably for the work of the ministry. Paul, therefore, would have Timothy "to go forth with him" (Acts 16:3).

Timothy willingly followed Paul and, because he was to be a missionary both to Jew and Gentile, he submitted to circumcision that he might conciliate the Jewish Christians and that his work among them might not be handicapped. He could follow the rite in good faith for his mother was a Jewess. He was ordained, no doubt, by the local council of presbyters in Derbe and Lystra.

Timothy set forth with Paul on the apostle's second missionary journey. He is specifically mentioned as being with Paul at Berea (Acts 17:13–14). We may, therefore, assume that he had accompanied Paul to all the places which the apostle visited prior to Berea. Because of the persecution at Berea, Paul chose to journey to Athens alone. He later summoned Timothy along with Silas to Athens, from whence they were immediately sent on an errand to the church in Thessalonica (1 Thess. 3:1–3). Paul departed from Athens before Timothy and Silas rejoined him. He then moved on to Corinth. There Timothy remained with Paul for a year and six months (Acts 18:11) until Paul continued his second missionary journey.

On Paul's third missionary journey Timothy was again his companion. This journey involved much travel and time. They spent more than two years at Ephesus. When Paul determined to go from Ephesus to Jerusalem, he sent Timothy and Erastus into Macedonia before him (Acts 19:22). When Paul wrote from Ephesus his first letter to Corinth, he mentioned that Timothy was to return to him from Corinth and bring to him a report on the condition of the Corinthian church (1 Cor. 4:17).

After the riot in Ephesus, Paul journeyed to Macedonia, and was joined by Timothy. From there they journeyed together to Greece, where they remained three months. When the apostle once more set his face toward Jerusalem, Timothy was with him.

After the apprehension of Paul in Jerusalem, the details

of Timothy's employment are not described until we find him once more with Paul during the apostle's first imprisonment in Rome. From this time forward, however, much is said about him. In three of Paul's epistles, written from Rome, he makes mention of Timothy (Col. 1:1; Philemon 1; Phil. 1:1). In Philippians 2:19 Paul says that he hopes to be able to send Timothy to visit the church at Philippi.

We are assuming that this hope was fulfilled, and that Paul was liberated, and once again Timothy was his traveling companion. It is impossible to trace the remaining journeys of Paul. We do know, however, that he left Timothy to represent him at Ephesus (1 Tim. 1:3). Not long thereafter Paul wrote the first epistle to Timothy, in which he gave careful instructions in regard to the manner in which the young pastor should conduct the affairs of the church at Ephesus until Paul should return (1 Tim. 3:14).

When Paul was imprisoned a second time, he felt that his trial would be followed by an adverse judgment and would issue in his death. He, therefore, wrote from Rome to Timothy at Ephesus, affectionately appealing to him to come to him. "Give diligence to come shortly unto me" (2 Tim. 4:9 ASV). How true and tender the affection was that bound Paul and Timothy together is reflected in the fact that when no Christian friend was with Paul save his beloved physician, Luke, it was for Timothy that the aged apostle longed most. We have no way of knowing whether or not Timothy arrived before Paul's execution.

John Rutherford has written:

Of all Paul's friends, with the exception, perhaps of Luke, Paul's beloved friend Timothy was regarded by him with the tenderest affection; he was his dearly beloved son, faithful and true. Various defects have been alleged to exist in Timothy's character. These defects are inferred from the directions and instructions addressed to him by Paul in the Pastoral Epistles, but these references may be wrong, and it is a mistake to exaggerate them in view of his unbroken and unswerving loyalty and of the long and faithful service rendered by him to Paul, "as a child serveth a father" (Philippians 2 : 22).[2]

## II. DATES AND DESTINATION

About A.D. 61, Paul was released from his first Roman imprisonment. It is fairly certain that he was martyred by Nero by A.D. 67. Many scholars believe that he was martyred in A.D. 64, in connection with the burning in Rome. Sometime between his release and his martyrdom he wrote 1 Timothy. There is evidence that 2 Timothy was written shortly before Paul's martyrdom. In this epistle Paul refers to himself as a prisoner (1:8, 16; 2:9). He is anticipating his death (4:6). This was the last of all of Paul's letters and was written before A.D. 67.

Both of the letters to Timothy were addressed to Ephesus, where Paul had left him to preach. Second Timothy was almost certainly written from Paul's second Roman imprisonment. We cannot be sure where Paul was when he wrote 1 Timothy.

---

[1] White, *The Expositor's Greek Testament* (London: Hodder & Stoughton, Ltd., 1917), IV, pp. 58-59. Used by permission.

[2] Rutherford, *International Standard Bible Encyclopedia* (Grand Rapids: Wm. B. Eerdmans Publishing Co., 1939), V, 2985. Used by permission.

# PART ONE

# 1 TIMOTHY

# CHAPTER 1

I. THE SALUTATION (1:1-2)
   1. The Writer
   2. The Recipient
   3. Words of Personal Greeting

II. APPEAL TO MAINTAIN SOUND DOCTRINE (1:3-7)
   1. Strategic City
   2. Doctrinal Confusion
   3. Centrality of Love
   4. Warning Against False Teachers

III. THE RELATION OF A CHRISTIAN TO THE LAW (1:8-11)
   1. Law and Grace
   2. Purpose of the Law
   3. The Gospel of Grace

IV. PAUL'S EXPERIENCE WITH CHRIST (1:12-17)
   1. Unwitting Sins of the Past
   2. God's Abundant Grace
   3. A Doxology

V. TIMOTHY APPOINTED PAUL'S SUCCESSOR (1:18-20)
   1. The Warfare
   2. The Warning

# 1

# Timothy Receives His Commission

IN THE LETTERS to Timothy, we have the wisdom of a great pastor whose work was to train pastors and provide leadership for the churches he had helped to establish. Soon he must leave these churches entirely in other hands. He was supremely concerned about those pastors who must follow him. He, therefore, in these epistles pours out his central conviction that the Christian church must ever have a well-trained, deeply devoted, and highly consecrated ministry.

Nothing is more emphasized in these letters to Timothy than the importance of being in constant touch with God through prayer and the study of the Word (1 Tim. 2:1, 8; 4:6, 12–16; 2 Tim. 1:3; 2:15, 22; 3:14–15).

The pastor must, first of all, nourish his own soul on the words of faith and good doctrine (1 Tim. 4:6). Then, he must teach and remind the brethren of the central things of our most holy faith. Practicing true godliness in their own pattern of conduct, they must bring the members of their congregation to do the same (1 Tim. 4:16). The total responsibility of the Christian pastor to his church members centers in and grows out of these grand centralities.

Obviously, much that is written to Timothy as a pastor is God's message to pastors throughout the whole church age. As the functioning of our churches has made it necessary to multiply the church staff of vocational workers and the number of volunteer workers in the organization, should we not apply, in principle, to all church leaders the standards set forth in the pastoral epistles?

## I. THE SALUTATION (1:1–2)

New Testament letters normally follow the pattern in vogue in ancient Greece. The name of the writer is given first and is followed by that of the recipient. Usually words of personal greeting are included along with good wishes for the reader's physical health. Paul obviously follows the traditional pattern in its main format; however, he expresses solicitude not for the physical but for the spiritual well-being of Timothy.

### 1. *The Writer*

Upon first reading Paul's salutation to Timothy, we may think that it appears a bit distant and formal and not at all what we would expect from one who had known this young man in the ministry so intimately. They had crossed many dividing seas together for Christ. Why then should Paul begin a letter in so formal a fashion as "Paul, an apostle of Jesus Christ by the commandment of God" (1:1)? It seems evident that it is not because Timothy had ever questioned Paul's apostleship.

Perhaps the apostle desired Timothy to remember that this was not a bit of casual correspondence. Paul thus introduces himself as "an apostle of Jesus Christ by the commandment of God" to emphasize the profound importance of his message. Paul was not in the ministry of his own choosing; he had heard a divine call and had been apprehended by divine hands. Nothing gives courage to a minister as does the assurance that he has been commissioned by a divine command.

"Apostle" literally means "one sent." In the Christian context he is one who is under divine orders to bear witness to the gospel of the life, death, and resurrection of the Redeemer. How much Paul stresses his spiritual authority in this first verse! He was an apostle of Jesus Christ, commissioned by Christ; he was in this position by the commandment of God; he was one who had committed himself to the leadership of Jesus Christ; and he was the bearer of the only message of hope.

The final foundation of our hope is in the redeeming reality of the intervention of God into our world in Jesus Christ as the only Saviour.

> None other Lamb, none other Name.
> None other Hope in heaven or earth or sea,
> None other Hiding-place from guilt and shame,
> None beside Thee.
>
> CHRISTINA ROSSETTI

## 2. The Recipient

It seems obvious that Timothy was Paul's closest and most devoted follower. Here Paul calls him "my own son in the faith" (1:2). Timothy was probably converted when Paul visited Lystra on his first missionary journey (Acts 14:6–20; 16:1–3). Paul had carefully nurtured the soul of his young friend until they were bound together with most invigorating and indissoluble bonds of faith and love. Writing to the church at Colossae, Paul greets them not only in his own name but also in the name of Timothy, "our brother" (Col. 1:1 ASV).

From the days of our Lord, the apostles worked together in twos. At the time this epistle was written, Timothy was closest to Paul, who calls him his brother, a term which has been baptized with Christian meaning and used to express that warm relationship which is created among Christians by the injection of the very life of God into their souls through the indwelling Christ, thus creating a closer bond than that of the ties of blood relationship in an earthly family.

How regrettable it is that we have allowed the term brother, which originally was one of the richest and most glorious words in the Christian vocabulary, to degenerate into a term of pious slang. We need to redeem this word from the depths into which it has fallen and let it again express that most blessed of relationships.

When Paul speaks of his "son in the faith" he means that while, as an apostle, he was the channel through whom the gospel was communicated to Timothy, it is to the gospel itself that Timothy owes his conversion and to which he must yield his allegiance. Nothing is more commendable in Paul's exercise of his apostolic authority than his careful insistence that both he and Timothy are under a common Master. Paul, therefore, never attempted personally to dominate Timothy, but to bring him into submission to Christ.

When Paul speaks of Timothy as his "own son in the faith" (1:2), he also is reminding him that the gospel is historically grounded. It is not the product of speculative thought, but is grounded in the concrete vortex of human history in Bethlehem, Calvary, and Olivet. The historic gospel stands in contrast with the "fables" (1:4) which seek constantly to infiltrate and distort the true gospel and which lure some Christians away from the central truth.

## 3. Words of Personal Greeting

"Grace, mercy, and peace" (1:2) compose a benediction which gives us a glimpse of the face of God. Grace speaks of the boundless, outgoing favor of God which is grounded solely in his love. Mercy suggests God's constant desire and readiness to forgive. Peace suggests the state of a man who is reconciled with God.

Few things are more pathetic today than our distortion of this most wondrous gift of God, by which we reduce our religion to a peace-of-mind cult. In the New Testament "peace" means that state of reconciliation with God which makes possible and real our reconciliation with men of good will. No man can be at peace with God's creation until, first of all, he is at peace with God, and by the same token, no man can be at peace with God who is out of fellowship with the people of God.

## II. Appeal to Maintain Sound Doctrine (1:3–7)

This passage stresses the heavy emphasis Paul placed upon stabilizing the early Christian churches in their understanding and practice of true Christian doctrine. Paul's appeal for Timothy to abide at Ephesus was, no doubt, predicated on Timothy's desire to be engaged in the more romantic endeavor of traveling with Paul.

### 1. Strategic City

The apostle, however, saw that nothing was more important than stabilizing the strategic congregation in Ephesus. Not only was Ephesus the chief city of Asia Minor and the seat of the proconsul of the province, it was also a great commercial center of wealth, connecting a vast system of roads. Furthermore, many vigorous religious cults which strongly resisted the Christian invasion had their headquarters in Ephesus. Here the Roman Emperor was worshiped most devotedly. Here was the renowned temple of Artemis, or Diana (Acts 19:24ff.). Many magic arts were practiced here.

The importance of the city is seen in the fact that it had known the ministry of Paul, Apollos, Aquila and Priscilla, as well as Timothy. Moreover, four letters in the New Testament are addressed to Ephesus. They are, besides the two epistles to Timothy, Paul's Ephesian letter and the one in Revelation 2:1–7. Tradition contends that Timothy, John, and Mary, the mother of Jesus, were buried in Ephesus.

## 2. Doctrinal Confusion

There can be no doubt that in the concepts of many of the people there was a mixture, or *syncretism*, of Jewish, pagan, and Christian doctrine, which sought to combine the teachings of the various religions, selecting only those beliefs common to all. Syncretism presented a chaotic and formidable confusion with which the Christian missionaries had constantly to do battle. When, therefore, Paul urges Timothy to "charge some that they teach no other doctrine" (1:3), he is calling him to remember that wherever heresy seeks to dilute the doctrine of the Christian faith, the herald of the cross must resolutely withstand it.

That there was a clearly defined body of doctrine to which the early church adhered is reflected in Paul's appeal to Timothy to make sure that no different doctrine was taught. In the New Testament the word translated "to teach different doctrine" occurs only here (1:3) and in 1 Timothy 6:3. It means to deviate from the normative standard of Christian faith.

Paul further entreats Timothy to see to it that teachers in the church did not become enamored with fables or myths, which were imaginative, untrue accounts of religious experiences (1:4). They were "endless" in the sense that unrestrained fancy never terminates in anything definite and concrete. The "fables" were the products of a morbid craving for controversy which has perpetually plagued the church. The "endless genealogies" were those allegorical interpretations of the Old Testament which Jewish Christians had employed to make the Old Testament sit in judgment upon the New Testament. They refused to allow the New Testament to be the final interpretation and fulfilment of the Old Testament.

This approach, Paul knew, caused speculation and quarreling. He also knew that Christianity is a gospel of action rather than speculation and that many who bear the name of Christian often prefer to substitute speculation about doctrine for service for Christ. Speculation and debate are ruthless destroyers of Christian fellowship. Men are never argued into the kingdom of Christ. Argument only serves to defend one's personal point of view and to minister to one's pride of intellect. It often ends in one's lying in defense of the truth and hating in defense of love.

On the other hand, "godly edifying" builds up Christian character that is grounded "in faith" by which the divine revelation is received. The basic difference between all pagan religion and the Christian faith is that the former is grounded in the endless speculations of men, which can never arrive at ultimate spiritual reality, and the latter is grounded in the final revelation of God, who has made himself fully known in Jesus Christ.

### 3. *Centrality of Love*

The end or purpose of Paul's appeal is not to stir up further controversy in the church by antagonizing these false teachers, but rather to create love for them and in them, love which flows not out of a fanatical devotion to abstract doctrines or statements of faith, but rather out of a pure heart or a sound moral character and out of a good conscience. Sound doctrine cannot flow out of a love which is nothing more than sentimental feeling. It can flow only out of a heart wholly given to the purposes of God.

Again, Paul says that Christian love must be grounded in a good conscience (1:5). In other words, the innate faculty by which man judges right and wrong must be constantly assuring him that his course of conduct is right, otherwise Christian love cannot abide in his heart. Moreover, Paul says that Christian love must be grounded in unfeigned, sincere faith. From the divine side faith is the gift of divine love. From the human side faith is the channel which lets the divine love flow through. In essence, all of these expressions combine to say that Christian love is the product, not of clever disputation, but of purehearted, conscientious, and sincere committal to the revelation manifested in Jesus Christ and communicated through the apostles. Such love has a central place in sound doctrine.

### 4. *Warning Against False Teachers*

Those who had "swerved," or literally had "missed the mark," had allowed their gospel to degenerate into "vain jangling," or empty argument (1:6). Such teachers had used the law most destructively. It is difficult to know what is meant by "teachers of the law" in this context (1:7). Paul could conceivably be using the term ironically to indicate that these false teachers who were disturbing the faith of the church were caught in the contradiction of pretending to return to Judaism while continuing on in the Christian church. On the other hand, he may be saying that their failure to understand the Christian interpretation of the law disqualifies them as teachers in the Christian church.

### III. THE RELATION OF A CHRISTIAN TO THE LAW (1:8–11)

Few questions are more transcendently important for a Christian than the question concerning the place of the law in the Christian faith.

### 1. *Law and Grace*

Many Christians today still misconstrue the doctrine of grace, making it mean that God has lowered his stern and rigid moral requirements by abrogating the law and replacing it with an attitude of indifference toward the moral quality of a man's life. Nothing is clearer, however, in the Sermon on the Mount than our Lord's insistence that he came "not to destroy, but to fulfil" (Matt. 5:17 ASV). That is, he came to carry the law to its highest expression and to provide grace to enable us to obey the law. In truth, grace lays heavier moral demands upon us than the details of the Jewish law could ever require. Grace is that which is most characteristic of the moral nature of God, which demands that we be more Godlike than any law can describe, and which in turn provides the transforming dynamic and power for fulfilling the divine demands.

## 2. *Purpose of the Law*

"The law is good," says Paul, "if a man use it lawfully" (1:8). The law was never intended to be an instrument by which man, through moral obedience, could lift himself to God. Rather was it provided as a revealer of our inadequacies, to show us how far short we have fallen and to cause us to cast ourselves on the grace of God, which alone can deliver us. The law is bad when unlawfully used. It is bad for the man who cannot obey it, for it plunges him into despair. It is even worse, however, for the man who supposes he can obey it, for it produces in him the worst form of pride, the pride of goodness, and pride is the worst of sins.

Paul, therefore, insists that "the law is not made for a righteous man" (1:9). There should come a time in the life of every good man when he no longer has to debate whether or not he will refrain from murder, profanity, adultery, lying, theft, kidnaping, and all such abominable deviations from commendable moral conduct.

These sins are not temptations to a good man. These are so glaringly at variance with the teaching of the Christian faith that they should be finally settled forever in a Christian's pattern of conduct. These fundamental laws are posted to restrain the lawless and disobedient who refuse the authority of God over their lives.

All of these deviations are radically at variance with the

very nature of the Christian way of life which is described as "sound doctrine" (1:10). The word "sound" means healthful, or health-giving. True Christian doctrine is simply a description of the only way life will really work. The unfortunate thing about a man who rebels against this way is that he comes to the end of his life to find that he has never really lived. He has existed, but he has not known anything which is worthy to be called life.

### 3. *The Gospel of Grace*

Over against a dull negative declaration concerning man's common responsibilities, Paul places a "glorious gospel," a gospel which shines with the authentic radiance of heaven and brings the very glory of God into the soul of man (1:11). It is the "gospel of the blessed God," a God who is evermore worthy of being praised. Moreover, it is a gospel which, for all its glory, has been committed into the hands of Paul (and others) to be protected against false teachers and to be fervently propagated.

## IV. PAUL'S EXPERIENCE WITH CHRIST (1:12–17)

Paul was able to look back over a span of faithful devotion to Christ and to the true doctrine. He, therefore, thanks his Lord, for he knows full well that it is the enabling grace of God which has held him true to his mission (1:12). The measure of a man's character is reflected in that for which he is most grateful. Some are grateful for their immunity from sacrifice, struggle, and service. Paul was thankful for a mission which involved all of these and for the strength to fulfil his high calling.

### 1. *Unwitting Sins of the Past*

When Paul declares that he was counted faithful (v. 12) and then moves on to insist that he was a blasphemer, we are puzzled by an apparent contradiction. In the first statement there appears to be unseemly pride and in the second, exaggerated berating. Remember, however, that Paul, in the first instance, is talking about his trustworthiness, for even as a persecutor of Christians he was utterly sincere in believing that he was doing God a favor.

Paul's experience is a glaring example of the error of those who contend that it makes little difference what a man believes as long as he is sincere. Vicious fanatics are usually surpassingly sincere. Moreover, we must remember that when Paul declares that he "was before a blasphemer, and a persecutor, and injurious," he is speaking as a man who has realized the enormous difference that Christ makes in human experience (1:13).

Paul later declares himself to be the chief of sinners (1:15). It is well, however, to remember that no one else ever called Paul that. In truth, he stood at the highest peak of the moral superiority provided through rigid adherence to the strict pharisaic code. Paul is the perfect example of the truth that a very good moral man can do some very evil things when he is not united with the indwelling Christ, who alone can give adequate guidance and power to perform the will of God.

Paul knew that his Lord had put him into the ministry not because of any merit, for he had been guilty of blasphemy, the worst of offenses. He had consented to the death of Stephen and was a persecutor and murderer of the Christian martyrs. Yet as long as he was an unbeliever, Paul was ignorant of the consequences of his crimes. He, therefore, obtained mercy. The Old Testament makes a strong distinction between "presumptuous" sins and "unwitting" sins (Lev. 22:14; Num. 15:22–31). "Unwitting" sins are less blameworthy than "presumptuous" sins.

Unwittingly we continually do what the poet described:

These clumsy feet, still in the mire
  Go crushing blossoms without end;
These hard, well-meaning hands we thrust
  Among the heart-strings of a friend.[1]

                              EDWARD ROLAND SILL

Paul's unwitting sin was vastly different from the crime of the crucifiers. We have often misinterpreted the prayer of Jesus from his cross, "Father, forgive them; for they know not what they do" (Luke 23:34). It is the conviction of this writer that what Jesus was saying was that, because his enemies knew not that God would transcend this crime of crucifixion and use the cross for the redemption of the world (no thanks to the crucifiers) and because they were ignorant of any good that would come out of this cross, for them the crucifixion was nothing but the blackest of crimes. They were deliberately sinning, while Paul could say of his past sin, "I did it ignorantly in unbelief."

Nothing can cover the facts of the malicious deeds of men in the past. Jesus was never sentimental about the brutality of man's sin. He could never, therefore, say lightly, "Let bygones be bygones."

## 2. God's Abundant Grace

Neither did Paul look lightly upon his past. Only the "overflowing" grace of God could ever cover Paul's transgression. Nowhere in secular Greek writings nor in the Septuagint does the verb appear which is here translated "was exceeding abundant," or "abounded exceedingly" (1:14 ASV). Paul seems to be coining a word to express what had never been expressed before. It means that where sin had abounded, grace overflowed all the more. This was the overflowing grace of God which had produced faith and love in the heart of Paul as the indwelling Christ moved into the control room of his life.

At this point Paul calls to mind a familiar saying in the

early church. Perhaps it was a stanza of a well-loved hymn. "This is a faithful saying, and worthy of all acceptation, that Christ Jesus came into the world to save sinners" (1:15). Reflecting on his personal experience in the light of this saying, Paul concludes that never was the divine grace more active and adequate than when it saved the chief of sinners. The nearer any man is to Jesus Christ the more he feels the enormity of his sins.

Paul saw that the very purpose of Christ's coming was to redeem all men, even the worst of sinners. His redeeming Paul was for the purpose of demonstrating, to all who doubted that Paul could be saved, that the invitation of God's grace is open to all men. No man need be reluctant to come to Christ because of the greatness of his sin. In Paul, Christ first demonstrated the extent of his long-suffering patience with sinners. Thus the foremost sinner became the foremost pattern for all men of that life which is grounded in Christ and made real by our faith which unites us with Christ in the life eternal.

### 3. A Doxology

At this point Paul lifts up one of the two doxologies which appear in this epistle. The other is in 1 Timothy 6:15–16. Note the marginal reading given in the American Standard Version: "Now unto the King of the ages, incorruptible, invisible, the only God, be honor and glory unto the ages of the ages" (1:17).

Here Paul declares in beautifully balanced and profoundly significant language the supremacy of God who is the "King of the kingdom of redemption." He is "King eternal" or "King of the ages." The Jews had taken the concept of the ages over from the Babylonian idea that human history is divided into world periods, or thousand-year cycles which, in the heavenly order, correspond to our earthly years. Of all these heavenly cycles God is King.

God is also immortal or imperishable. His majesty is neither enhanced nor tarnished by time; neither is he limited by time. He transcends time and is not dependent upon the time sequence for his knowledge of the future. In his very nature God is the only God. In such sublime majesty he only is worthy of honor and glory forever and ever.

## V. TIMOTHY APPOINTED PAUL'S SUCCESSOR (1:18–20)

Paul's letter to Timothy is composed of a series of charges which appear to some scholars to be too rash and forbidding for Paul to deliver to a comrade so close and faithful as was Timothy. They contend that there is no evidence that Timothy was ever on the brink of apostasy. It should be remembered, however, that Paul's affection for Timothy was not so superficially sentimental that it had to be expressed in extravagant flattery. The aged apostle was, as it were, passing the torch to the young minister who would carry on the work of the gospel. Serious words of counsel and warning were needed for such a solemn charge as was being given to young Timothy, and to all the Timothy's who would, down through the ages, be called to places of leadership in Christian work.

### 1. *The Warfare*

In those difficult, stressful days every herald of the cross was engaged in constant conflict with forces which threatened to destroy the Christian faith, and so every herald needed clear warning against the perils of apostasy. Timothy was most assuredly not exempt from such a struggle. Furthermore, it may well be that Paul was thinking not only of the Timothy whom he knew so intimately but also of all the young Timothys whom God should afterward call into his service.

The charge to wage virile warfare and cling valiantly to the faith and a good conscience is grounded in the past, in that Timothy's call to the ministry was manifested in the work of the Holy Spirit and in the words of assurance from Christian prophets. This may mean that at the ordination of Timothy prophecies concerning his service for Christ were spoken. At any rate, the emphasis is upon the measure of Timothy's indebtedness to those who have gone before him. Who of us can ever comprehend his personal indebtedness to those inspiring influences which have poured out of the staunch loyalty and fervent zeal of the faithful believers who have served Christ before us and have passed on their commission to us?

## 2. The Warning

Timothy must not only take heart from the true servants of Christ in the past, he must also take warning from those who, through the repudiation of their professed faith and the violation of their conscience, have made shipwreck of their religion.

The Christian faith and a good conscience must walk hand in hand. Faith and conduct in the Christian religion are inextricably woven together. True faith creates a good conscience. To violate a good conscience is to repudiate the validity of one's faith. Conduct is the only adequate measure of what one truly believes.

Does this making shipwreck of faith indicate that those who have been so involved are lost? The New Testament emphasizes that there is only one kind of faith through which the grace of God may flow and unite the believer with Christ, and that is the faith which God himself creates by enabling man to respond in full committal now and forever to the will of God. The only faith through which man may be saved is the faith which has in it the quality of endurance. It endures as Christ dwells in the soul and keeps his creative, redeeming energy alive as he continually works to produce a Christlike nature. Faith which does not endure is not saving faith. If one makes shipwreck of his faith, he gives evidence that he has been trusting in his own power to cling to Christ rather than in Christ's power to quicken and keep alive one's faithful devotion and obedience to him.

A good warfare against evil cannot be waged apart from a faith which keeps the spiritual morale high and strong. This faith was specifically grounded in the truth which Timothy had received from those Christians who had gone before him. Neither can the battle against evil be won apart from a good conscience. If the conscience is troubled, there is evidence of a moral deficiency in one's faith. True saving faith must include the moral surrender of the will to the control of Christ. Obedience and faith are reciprocal in the experience of a Christian.

Specific persons are called to Timothy's mind as grim reminders of men who had made shipwreck of their faith. Their "delivery to Satan" is felt by many scholars to mean that they were disciplined for blasphemy by being excommunicated from the Christian congregation. That Paul used this method to bring them to repentance is indicated in the statement, "that they may learn not to blaspheme" (1:20). These men had played so fast and loose with conscience that the church had to withdraw fellowship from them that they might realize the enormity of their sin and duly repent thereof.

That Paul was filled with compassion even for such erring members becomes quite evident as we compare 1 Corinthians 5:1–5 with the further comment in 2 Corinthians 2:4–8.

## SUGGESTIONS FOR STUDY AND DISCUSSION

1. The teacher should invite the class to read 1 Timothy at one sitting before the second night of study and 2 Timothy before the third night of study.
2. Each member of the class should bring his New Testament to

the class, along with a notebook for preserving helpful comments.

3. Let each member of the class, as he reads, make his own list of qualifications of a good pastor. In the final period of study these may be discussed, summarized, and placed on the chalkboard.

4. Let each member make a list of the responsibilities of the church toward her pastor. These also may be discussed and placed on the chalkboard.

5. Consider the list of qualifications for pastors as you compile it during this study and carefully evaluate each quality as it applies to (1) other members of a church staff; (2) elected church officers; (3) Sunday school officers and teachers; (4) persons in places of leadership in other church organizations. From this study, formulate a statement of your belief about our New Testament authority for emphasizing teaching and training in the church program.

---

[1] Sill, "The Fool's Prayer," from the works of Edward Rowland Sill (Boston: Houghton Mifflin Co.).

# CHAPTER 2

I. THE GOSPEL FOR EVERY MAN (2:1–7)

    1. Prayer for All
    2. Salvation Available for All
    3. A Ransom Provided for All
    4. A Messenger to All

II. PROPER PROCEDURES FOR PUBLIC WORSHIP (2:8–15)

    1. Instructions to Men About Prayer
    2. Instructions to Women About Dress
    3. Woman's Role in Public Worship

# 2

# *Proper Procedures for Public Worship*

## I. THE GOSPEL FOR EVERY MAN (2:1–7)

With the weighty argument concerning his authority as a background, Paul moves on to counsel Timothy regarding his prayers. The measure of one's religion is reflected in the scope of his praying. True Christian prayer must embrace all of the needs of all classes and conditions of men. Even as the gospel has relevance for all men, so all men stand in need of the prayers of others. We can imagine how many times the early church had need of such prayer as they were beseiged on every hand by bitter persecution and as the false teachings of *syncretism* and *Gnosticism* built their invulnerable walls through which nothing less than the divine power could penetrate.

The Gnostics claimed superior knowledge of spiritual truths. They did not recognize Jesus Christ as equal with God. They taught that all that is material or physical is evil. Syncretism was seeking to unite all religions by choosing from each the points on which all religionists could agree. In contrast, Christianity was seeking the conquest of the world for Christ.

### 1. *Prayer for All*

The four words used to describe prayer—"supplications, prayers, intercessions, and giving of thanks" (2:1)—simply

represent Paul's endeavor to impress upon Timothy the necessity of running the whole gamut of prayer. Not only
supplications in grave crises but also steady, sustained
prayers and earnest intercessions—offered perhaps for those
who never pray for themselves—along with continual thanks-
giving, must be offered up before God.

The measure of a man's soul is in that for which he most
thanks God. If he thanks God most for material things—
food, raiment, automobiles, houses, and lands—he is a mate-
rialist. If he thanks God most for physical health, he is a
naturalist. If he thanks God most for his spiritual blessings,
he is rising higher on the scale of existence but may still be
supremely self-centered. It is only when a man may thank
God supremely for God himself that he is of all men most
blessed, for then he is assured that having God (or being
had by God) he shall most assuredly have all things else.

One of the greatest omissions in the worship of many of
our churches is the failure to pray for those who live in that
fierce light that shines on public officials. Says Paul, "It is
the will of God that all should share the heavy burdens of
those who must exercise authority, by praying for them." [1]
Christian churches must never be so concerned with any one
class of men that they overlook the spiritual needs of all
men—even our national and community leaders, who because of their heavier responsibilities have heavier needs.

The way to a quiet, peaceable, honest, and godly life is
the way of prayer. Only as we pray for our public officials
and as they in turn are given divine guidance and power
may we know peaceable life. It is sin in the hearts of men
that leads to a situation in which people fight because one
is ready and the other is not. The final eradication of war
cannot depend upon preparedness to fight. Personal and
international strife can be dissolved only through that sincere good will which leads us to desire and pray for nothing

but the best for all men under heaven and especially for those who have the rule over us.

Verse 3 is Paul's answer to the hesitancy of Christians to pray for pagan rulers. Although the worship of the emperor was rigidly enforced in Ephesus, Christians steadfastly refused to bow before him. The apostle's word is that Christians must pray not *to* the emperor but *for* him, for he was a man like other men and, therefore, needed salvation. The fact that Christians are called upon to pray for kings means that kings are called upon to seek salvation through Christ. Paul insists that "this is good and acceptable in the sight of God our Saviour" (2:3). Because the rulers were persecuting the church and seeking to subdue the religion of Jesus Christ, they stood all the more in need of God's transforming grace, which could find an entrance into their souls through the prayers of others. It is the desire of God that even such arch persecutors of the church should be saved. Who could know this better than Paul?

## 2. Salvation Available for All

Through prayer comes not only salvation, but also "the knowledge of the truth" (2:4). The knowledge of the truth is bound up with a personal experience of salvation. Knowledge in the higher level comes not so much from speculation and rationalization as through repentance and faith, and ultimately through a committal to him who is the Truth.

Since there is but one God, he must be for all men. The man Christ Jesus is the only Mediator between God and man. Communion with God and knowledge of him comes through the mediatorial work of the Redeemer. Only in this passage and in Hebrews does the New Testament speak of Christ as the Mediator. This term is used to refute the popular conception among many religions that there are numerous mediators between God and man. To the Jews, Moses and the law, the high priest, and angels were mediators. In the Gnostic systems "aeons" were the mediators through which the "high good God" could touch the defiling earth and still remain personally undefiled.

But Paul contends that Christ is the only Mediator. He does not mean that Christ is an intermediate being in the sense that he stands between God and man. He is rather the One who is wholly identified with God and man, thus bringing the two together by bringing man into his fellowship through faith and thus bringing him to God. The idea is not that we go through Christ and out beyond him into the vast unknown to get to God, rather is it that when we get to Christ we get to God. All that we may ever know of God must be known in Christ.

Paul's emphasis on "the man Christ Jesus" is made as a refutation of the argument of certain heretics who did not accept the full humanity of Jesus (2:5). There were a group of the Gnostics (Docetics) who argued that the body of Jesus was not truly a human body but only a vehicle to manifest his humanity. It is significant that many of the earliest skeptics did not inveigh against the deity of Christ, but against his humanity. For them it was not difficult to believe that one who had lived as Jesus lived, loved as Jesus loved, spoken as Jesus spoke, and died as Jesus died was more than man. Their great difficulty was in believing that he was really a man. The New Testament, therefore, lays emphasis upon his essential manhood. Jesus is God who became man that he might lift us through our union with him into the fellowship of God.

## 3. *A Ransom Provided for All*

Paul's insistence that Christ gave himself a ransom for all recalls the statement of Jesus in Mark 10:45: "For even the Son of man came not to be ministered unto, but to minister, and to give his life a ransom for many." Jesus was probably dwelling on the question in Mark 8:37, "What shall a man give in exchange for his soul?" In the mind of our Lord, when a man had forfeited his soul there was no human means of buying it back.

The word "ransom," in the Greek world of the first century, was used to denote the amount of money necessary to purchase the freedom of a slave. The ransom which Christ paid is for all, including kings. All men are bought with a price. The testimony of this truth took place when Jesus gave himself in decisive redemptive action in God's determined time on the cross.

### 4. A Messenger to All

Paul had been ordained to bear witness of the redeeming, reconciling work of Christ. The three phases of the apostle's ministry, as aptly drawn together under three titles, are preacher, apostle, and teacher (2:7). As a preacher he was called to convey the gospel in an authoritative, solemn, compelling proclamation which would call forth the respect of his hearers. As an apostle, he was a messenger sent to herald the good tidings of God's redeeming grace in Christ wherever the Spirit directed him. As a teacher, he must interpret the meaning of the Christian faith and apply it to the practical problems immediately before him and his people. Moffat's translation of this passage, "to teach the Gentiles faith and truth," conveys the meaning most clearly and is in harmony with the tone of the entire epistle.[2]

## II. Proper Procedures for Public Worship (2:8–15)

Paul now turns from his emphasis on the universal validity of prayer through the only Mediator to describe the proper procedures in public worship. The word translated "I will" or "I desire" carries a twofold emphasis (2:8). It indicates the writer's authority, and it magnifies the need for that which is about to be written.

### 1. *Instructions to Men About Prayer*

The insistance that men should pray in every place may imply that this conventional practice was being altered to permit women to participate in leading public prayer. It was quite natural that the liberating power of the gospel was rapidly elevating women to their rightful position. The Spirit of God is no respecter of sex. Women have played a vital role in the church from its inception. In Paul's day, however, their leading in public prayer would have subjected them to the criticism which would fall upon any woman who was conspicuous in public.

In the ancient East women were secluded in their homes. It would have been a violation of all propriety for them to be so brazen as to speak in public. This passage cannot be taken as the universal directive of Paul for all time to come, but as the immediate handling of a local problem. It is more than obvious that Paul did not seek to exclude women from the work of the church. In his epistles he mentions the names of women who were widely known for their work in the church. Among them were Lydia, Dorcas, Priscilla, Tryphaena and Tryphosa, Persis, Julia, Euodia, and Syntyche.

Nevertheless, Paul is clear in his insistence that the primary responsibilities in the church must be carried by men. Foremost among these responsibilities was the leading of public prayer. The most prevalent posture for prayer was standing with the arms stretched out with the palms upward in anticipation of receiving a gift from above. The "lifting up holy hands" (2:8) denotes the need for moral cleansing as one approaches God in prayer. In the Jewish worship, such cleansing was symbolized by a ritual of washing the hands. This form of praying must include not only a posture which signified the fulfilment of the prerequisite of cleansing and faithful anticipation, but also a heart at peace with one's neighbors.

Only those who have forgiven others can experience forgiveness. This truth is reminiscent of our Lord's words in the Sermon on the Mount: "Therefore if thou bring thy gift to the altar, and there rememberest that thy brother hath ought against thee; leave there thy gift before the altar, and go thy way; first be reconciled to thy brother, and then come and offer thy gift" (Matt. 5:23-24).

## 2. *Instructions to Women About Dress*

Paul even speaks specifically about the manner of dress for women attending worship. It is interesting to note that Paul commands women to "adorn" themselves for worship (2:9). There is nothing in his command to encourage the defacing of womanly beauty. The word he uses means "to decorate, embellish, arrange in order." This would certainly include the enhancing of true feminine beauty. In truth, it is the very word from which we derive our word "cosmetics." It could, therefore, not be taken to encourage those sects who think it spiritual to veil or deface the most lovely of God's creations.

Paul says that women should adorn themselves, but remember that "modesty" is the best adornment. He is appealing for spiritual good taste, which does not accentuate the sensual but magnifies the simplicity which attends all true beauty. The word translated "shamefacedness" in the King James Version is more correctly rendered "discreetness."

The warning against ostentations pretense in worship through parading one's gold or pearls or costly array seems to argue for the presence of some wealth at this time in the church. Women were to guard against distracting from worship through the gaudy display of themselves. "The adornment with which women are to be chiefly concerned," says Paul, "is the adornment of good works." These good works are tokens of genuine Christianity, while the parading of oneself is pretentious paganism.

### 3. Woman's Role in Public Worship

Women are frankly enjoined to "learn in silence" (2:11). It should be borne in mind that Paul's problem was the perennial problem of adjusting ideal Christian morality into the framework of existing social customs. In an age when respectable women never ventured unveiled outside of their houses, when only courtesans were unveiled in public, it was not too much to ask Christian women to avoid criticism by suppressing their impulses to speak in public worship. Although, from the spiritual standpoint, in Christ there is neither "male nor female," the proprieties of the age demanded that women not use their freedom in a way to handicap the onward march of the gospel. Woman's role in the public worship of that day was to be that of the learner, not that of the teacher.

In verse 13, Paul uses the Genesis account of creation to establish the primacy of man and to point out that it was through Eve that Adam fell. The first time that woman taught man was when Eve taught Adam to eat the forbidden fruit.

This word about primacy sounds like woefully archaic advice. Yet many of our best counselors are reminding us today that man must be the head of his home if the home is to be stable. The physical side of marriage reaches its fulfilment as husband and wife recognize their basic differences. In one sense a marriage must be a partnership, but in the most intimate interpersonal relationships, Paul said, "Wives submit yourselves unto your own husbands" (Eph. 5:22). He meant by that to emphasize that only in this manner may woman fulfil her own true function.

Man was made by nature to initiate the physical relationships of marriage and woman was made to respond, to submit. The dominant role of the male on the physical level is thus rooted in the creative process and is exemplified in the sexual relationship. To talk about equality between men and women at this point is nonsense. It is the very difference between man and woman that makes possible the continuance of the creative process.

Paul saw this truth most profoundly. Woman's true fulfilment is in her devotion to that for which she was created, the bearing and rearing of children. When the Lord leads a woman to be a homemaker, wife, and mother, she may well believe that to keep the home and to "continue in faith and charity and holiness with sobriety" is a loftier work for her even than being a leader in the church.

## SUGGESTIONS FOR STUDY AND DISCUSSION

1. Discuss Paul's counsel to Timothy concerning the scope of his prayers.
2. Let some of the class members suggest why pastors and church leaders are in greater need of prayer than other members of the church.
3. List some reasons why the primary responsibilities in the early church had to be carried by men.

---

[1] At many points the author gives his own translation or paraphrase of the Scripture passage.

[2] All quotations from Moffatt are taken from *The Bible: A New Translation by James Moffatt,* copyright 1922, 1935, and 1950 by Harper & Brothers, and are used by permission of Harper & Brothers.

# CHAPTER 3

I. QUALIFICATIONS FOR A PASTOR (3:1–7)
1. The Pastor's Office
2. The Pastor's Characteristics
3. The Pastor's Family Life

II. QUALIFICATIONS FOR DEACONS (3:8–13)
1. Warnings
2. Convictions and Conduct
3. The Wives
4. The Deacon's Family Life

# 3

# *Qualifications for Pastors and Deacons*

IN THE PLAN of God, he has permitted the very coming of his kingdom to be largely related to and dependent upon the relationship which a Christian congregation sustains to her pastor and with the measure of devotion with which a pastor discharges his duties toward his congregation. Few subjects can be more important for Christians to consider than the specific teachings of the Scriptures concerning the pastor's responsibility to his congregation and, in turn, the congregation's responsibility to the pastor.

## I. QUALIFICATIONS FOR A PASTOR (3:1-7)

Inasmuch as the title, bishop, has grown into a technical description of a position in the organizational structure of other denominations, and inasmuch as these structures represent a departure from the simple congregational forms of church government observed in the early churches, we prefer to translate *episkopēs* according to its earliest meaning, "overseer," or "guardian of souls"—one who watches over their welfare. Baptists, in general, prefer to designate those who are called to lead the local congregations pastors or undershepherds. Christ, being the Good Shepherd (John 10:14) and the Chief Shepherd (1 Peter 5:4), is our model. In the Scriptures the people of God are often likened to flocks of sheep.

## 1. *The Pastor's Office*

Contrary to the twisted modern concept that one who is called should fight furiously against the call of God into the ministry, Paul insists that if a man aspires to the ministry he "desireth a good work" (3:1). It is very difficult to imagine, as some have suggested, that some men of Paul's day were aspiring to be pastors because of the honor or prestige involved. Pastors must stand between their people and a hostile world and would be the first to suffer when persecution fell. Their material compensation would be negligible and their duties demanding and often embarrassing. Nothing could lead men into the pastorate and sustain them in its duties save the call of God and the assurance that they were engaged in a noble work for the eternal welfare of humanity. Paul, therefore, lays emphasis solely upon the work to which a man is invited when he is called into the ministry. His call from God and the challenge of his task must be the only lures into the ministry. His sole purpose must be measured in terms of the prayer of Ignatius of Loyola:

> Teach us, good Lord, to serve Thee as Thou deservest; to give and not count the cost; to fight and not heed the wounds; to toil and not to seek for rest; to labor and not ask for any reward, save that of knowing that we do Thy will. Amen! [1]

## 2. *The Pastor's Characteristics*

The great apostle lays heavy emphasis upon a disciplined life for the pastor. He knew that robust health is highly desirable in the work of the ministry. Few men can survive for long the heavy strain of the ministry without enormous physical and spiritual reserve.

Paul counsels the pastor to be temperate in food and drink and to practice moderation and balance in all legitimate forms of pleasure (1 Tim. 3:1–3). He counsels neither ascetic denial nor unbridled liberty in the enjoyment of pleasures.

Paul says specific things about the man who would be a Christian pastor. He must be blameless; above reproach; irreprehensible; one against whom no charge has, in point of fact, been brought; not inviting public criticism and thus dishonoring the church. He must be "the husband of one wife" (3:2). There has been continual debate concerning whether this is simply the prohibition of polygamy or whether it would include the forbidding of digamy—the right to marry after the death of one's wife—or whether it forbids both.

In the light of Paul's encouragement of young widows to remarry and his denunciation of those who forbid marriage (1 Tim. 4:3), and in the further light of the noble position which the family occupies in the whole of the New Testament, this writer believes that this passage inveighs against the asceticism which argues that celibacy is a higher estate than marriage. The passage, in principle, encourages the pastor to engage in Christian marriage, the union of one man with one woman for life. Certainly, the passage must be interpreted in the light of Christ's teaching about divorce (Matt. 19:3-12).

A pastor should be sober-minded and discreet, poised, balanced, and self-controlled. He should be of good behavior in the sense that a well-bred man must be well-behaved, orderly, and unruffled in times of tension, so that he may work harmoniously with people. He must be hospitable. Public lodgings were few and poorly kept in the first century. Christian evangelists were often on the move. Christians were all of one family. The home of every Christian, therefore, had to be open to every other Christian. The pastor was to be an example of this hospitality, for houses were the first meeting places of the church.

Strong emphasis is also placed upon the necessity for a pastor to be a teacher, that he might keep his congregation well-informed and grounded in the faith. There is ample New Testament authority for looking upon the pastor as the leader in the teaching and training ministry of the church. Arthur Flake stressed this obligation of the pastor.

> One of the New Testament qualifications of a pastor is that he must be "apt to teach" (1 Tim. 3:2). He is also enjoined to "commit the word to faithful men who are able to teach others also" (2 Tim. 2:2). . . . Evidently the pastor should teach and train the leaders in his church. This duty is a part of his work as a pastor of the church and he cannot transfer this obligation to others and at the same time fulfil his mission in the highest degree.[2]

"Not given to much wine" may be translated "no drunkard" (3:3). The pastor's self-control of his appetites must be an example for his people. He must not be violent nor quarrelsome.

There are records in the early church called "The Apostolic Constitution" which required that:

> A bishop, elder or deacon who strikes believers when they sin or unbelievers when they do wrong, desiring by such means to terrify them, we command to be deposed; for nowhere has the Lord taught us to do such things. On the contrary, when He was struck, He did not strike back, when He was reviled, He did not revile in return, when He suffered, He did not threaten.[3]

Would not the modern counterpart be the pastor who presides like a demagogue over his congregation and who vents his hostility on his congregation from the pulpit at frequent intervals? This is the man who lacks courage to face a member of his congregation forthrightly and personally with his accusations against him, choosing rather to hide his cowardice behind a pulpit and striking when the worshiper cannot strike back.

The pastor must not be greedy for base gain. That is, he must be free from an obsession for getting money. If money becomes the chief motive behind a pastor's ministry, he manifests that he is not truly trusting in the God whom he calls upon others to trust to supply all his needs.

Moreover, the pastor must be gentle, not contentious, for it is only the truly strong and assured who can afford to be gentle and to give ground. Again, Paul warns that a pastor must not have his heart set on money. Twice he warns against centering one's ministry around money. In Hebrews 13:5, the writer uses this identical word of warning and adds, "Be content with such things as ye have: for he hath said, I will never leave thee, nor forsake thee." Above all others, the pastor should be content in the thought that he is in the care and keeping of Christ, who is his constant companion and who has pledged to supply all his needs.

### 3. *The Pastor's Family Life*

The apostle lays heavy emphasis upon the pastor's care of his children. He must rear a respectful family, one which out of love acknowledges his authority. This pattern of love is absolutely essential because so much of the Christian gospel moves around the family relationships. If a pastor's family is disorderly, then the gospel he preaches is vitiated, or set at nought, by his example.

For instance, the Christian gospel calls God "Father." This name speaks of his boundless yet intimate love for his own. However, it also speaks of his supreme authority, for the Oriental father was the absolute sovereign in his family. God the Father's authority is grounded in his love. It is nevertheless unbending authority.

Furthermore, in the Christian vocabulary Jesus is regarded as our "Elder Brother." If the relationships of children in the home are not brotherly, this phase of the gospel is vitiated. Since the gospel thinks of heaven as the eternal home, if a pastor's home is not an ideal of joy and blessedness, this analogy also is robbed of significance.

The best home is one in which the children are not bludgeoned into submission but are so fully convinced of the love of their parents that they desire to bow to their authority. If a pastor's children are so little convinced of his love for them that they have no desire to obey him, how can he convince the church members of his love, or hope that they may in turn accord him the only authority which any pastor may truly have, the authority of superior love?

Paul also warns against the perils involved in making a "novice," or a recent convert, a pastor of a church (3:6). The word literally means a "newly planted" one. In an age when converts were pouring into the church out of paganism, it was highly precarious to place those enthusiastic but untrained men in places of responsibility. Does not this word also imply our need for trained workers today?

The word translated "pride" comes from a term whose primary meaning is smoke or vapor. It refers, therefore, to that conceit which befogs and clouds the understanding in matters in which a man himself is concerned. The conceit which is created by the applause and approval of a flattering congregation often brings the downfall of a young preacher for, being unable to withstand the furor of popular approval, he brings the condemnation or punishment of the devil upon himself.

Finally, it is urged that the pastor must have "a good report of them which are without" (3:7). Just as Paul had called upon the Christians at Thessalonica to command the respect of outsiders (1 Thess. 4:12) and upon those at Corinth to "give no occasion of stumbling, either to Jews, or to Greeks (1 Cor. 10:32 ASV), even so does he call upon pastors to see to it that they are well regarded by the community outside of the church. A religion which, in its very essence, was a repudiation of the world did not need proponents who were personally so obnoxious to those whom they addressed that their gospel was refused a hearing. To call to a church a pastor who invites the hostility of men is to bring him into an unbearable reproach, which is the devil's snare for thwarting the work of the church.

## II. QUALIFICATIONS FOR DEACONS (3:8–13)

Paul held no double standard for pastors and deacons. When he says, "Likewise must the deacons . . ." (3:8), he is gathering up everything he has said in verses 2 through 7 and insisting that it must apply also to deacons.

### 1. *Warnings*

Inasmuch as it was expected that deacons should be constantly visiting in the homes of the people, the vices against which Paul warns them were those to which they might easily fall victim. Wine was the common beverage of the Eastern world of the first century. It probably was served as we would serve coffee or tea to guests in the home. Since wine was used to refresh and stimulate a visitor, deacons might easily have their conversation accelerated thereby to the point of gossip. In the spirit of good fellowship, desiring to please, they might even fall prey to the double tongue, saying one thing to one person and something else to another.

Deacons must be neither receptacles nor vehicles of slander. They, therefore, are warned not to be "given to much wine" and not to become loose in their talk and give way to frivolity, forgetting the gravity of their visit. Deacons must, on the contrary, be serious, dignified, and earnest.

Furthermore, the deacon's example must not ensnare into the deadly clutches of alcohol men for whom Christ died. The better the man who drinks, the stronger is his influence on others to drink.

Dr. Ralph Sockman, in *How to Believe,* wrote:

> One clear, cold March day I stood at the edge of Niagara Falls. The cataract was garbed in her most glorious winter garments. The rapids above the falls sparkled in the afternoon sun. Some birds were swooping down to snatch a drink from the clear water. My host told me how he had seen birds carried over the brink. They had dipped down for a drink and ice had

formed on their wings. Then they had dipped for another drink and more ice weighed their little bodies. Another dip or two and they could not rise. Over the falls they went. Sin is as deceptive as the sparkling water of Niagara's wintry rapids. Dip into it once too often and we are not able to lay aside every weight and sin which clings so closely.[4]

This danger is especially true of drinking. Christ loved even alcoholics enough to die for them. A deacon must, therefore, remember that if Christ was willing to die for the alcoholics, a Christian must refrain from setting before anyone a temptation that can lead to so devastating a calamity as the wrecking of a life and the shattering of a home through compulsive drinking.

The warning that deacons must not be "greedy of filthy lucre" (3:8), or greedy for gain, is especially relevant. From the beginning deacons have gathered the offerings of the church, not only publicly but from house to house. In a day when all Christians were under heavy financial pressure, it was no doubt a strong temptation to deacons to withhold some of that which they had collected. Dr. Moffatt, therefore, translates the passage, "not . . . pilfering."

Have you ever realized how dependent the average church is upon the character of the deacons for her material support? Even with the finance committee of the modern church program, it is often the character and example of the deacons which, in large measure, encourages the congregation to give generously and to have confidence in the financial program of the church.

The modern temptation would not be for the deacon to pilfer, but to use his position to a financial advantage. There have been deacons who have become deeply offended because they were not given business from the church. Money, of itself, is not filthy; but when money is sought where none is due, it becomes filthy. The deacon's true position is one from which to give not to get.

## 2. Convictions and Conduct

The deacon is also under obligation to hold the "mystery of the faith in a pure conscience" (3:9). Christian faith must quicken and train the conscience until the conscience becomes the voice of God. This passage indicates that faith and conduct are vitally related. A deacon must have the law of heaven written upon his heart. His conscience must bear record that his Christian convictions and his conduct agree.

Paul tells us plainly that those being considered for election as deacons must have their characters thoroughly examined before they are approved. They must be "blameless" or above reproach in the sense that they are free from the faults described in the preceding verses.

## 3. The Wives

There is much division as to whether verse 11 is a reference to deacon's wives or to a parallel office of deaconness. Some scholars contend that the adverb "likewise," if we are to be consistent with verse 8, must be regarded as introducing another category of church officials known as deaconnesses, whom they believe performed for the women of the church the same sort of services that its deacons did for the men. Other scholars maintain that inasmuch as the qualifications mentioned here are too brief to describe a separate class of church officials, and since women officials are described in full in 5:9–16, the reference here is to wives.

We cannot tell from the word itself which is meant. The word literally means "women." The meaning must be determined from the context. It seems very plausible to interpret this passage in the light of the fact that deacon's wives who made pastoral visits with their husbands would easily fall prey to the temptations to gossip and over-indulgence in drink and would, therefore, need to be warned against these. Where deacons handled church monies, their wives would also share in the responsibility of guarding the money given through them to the church, and must refrain from laying greedy hands upon it.

### 4. The Deacon's Family Life

The deacons must follow the same high pattern of family life as the pastor. For all of this, the deacons receive rich rewards. First of all, they receive a good standing of true spiritual prestige. Through faithful service in their office there comes great spiritual enrichment. Through their devotion to their many responsibilities, they make steady progress in the faith and will find increasing joy and confidence in it.

Furthermore, they develop great boldness in the faith which is in Christ Jesus. Two of the early deacons, Philip and Stephen, were bold evangelists. The higher the deacon, or any other Christian, moves on the ladder of spiritual living, the greater confidence he has in sharing his faith. He is to confidently proclaim through word and deed the liberating grace of God until his soul glows with the reality of it.

Finally, Paul's word translated "good standing" (3:13 ASV), may mean that in the hour of death and judgment the faithful deacon's service will be acceptable before God. We ought always to remember that the first Christian martyr was Stephen, a deacon who died beneath a hail of stones.

Stephen was not the last deacon to be stoned in public. We are so often rude, unthoughtful, and unkind to those who serve the church. Deacons have often been stoned from the pulpit by panicky preachers who vent their hostility in public, and it is a sight to make the angels weep.

When Deacon Stephen died, he saw Christ standing! Do you see the symbolism? Christ is commonly depicted as sitting at the right hand of the Father. He is told, "Sit thou on my right hand, till I make thine enemies thy footstool" (Matt. 22:44). But Stephen saw him standing. The implication is that Christ could not sit still and see a deacon stoned. He rose to vindicate him, to go forth to meet him, and to receive him into the courts of his presence forever.


## SUGGESTIONS FOR STUDY AND DISCUSSION

1. Let the class members suggest the qualifications for a good pastor (1 Tim. 3:1–7) and place them on the chalkboard.
2. Let the class members suggest the qualifications for deacons (1 Tim. 3:8–13) and place them on the chalkboard.

[1] Ignatius Loyola, prayer quoted in *The Interpreter's Bible* (Nashville: Abingdon Press, 1955).

[2] Arthur Flake, *Sunday School Officers and Their Work* (Nashville: Convention Press, 1956), pp. 14-15.

[3] Alexander Roberts and James Donaldson, eds., "The Apostolic Constitution," *The Ante-Nicene Fathers* (New York: Charles Scribner's Sons, 1899), VII, p. 501. Used by permission.

[4] Ralph W. Sockman, *How to Believe* (New York: Doubleday & Co., Inc., 1953), pp. 178-179. Reprinted by permission of publisher.

# CHAPTER 4

I. THE CUSTODIAN OF THE CHRISTIAN MYSTERY (3:14–16)

    1. The Transmission of the Truth
    2. An Early Christian Hymn

II. WARNINGS AGAINST HERESY (4:1–5)

    1. The False Teachers
    2. Their False Attitude Toward Asceticism

III. CHARACTERISTICS OF A GOOD MINISTER (4:6–10)

    1. Instructing the Brotherhood
    2. Refusing Myths and Speculations
    3. Exercising Self-discipline
    4. Laboring and Trusting

IV. CHARACTER ABOVE CHRONOLOGY (4:11–16)

    1. The Pastor's Conduct
    2. The Pastor's Use of the Scriptures
    3. The Exercise of the Pastor's Gift

# 4

# *Characteristics of a Good Minister*

IN THE MIDST of much stern and heavy admonition, Paul now pauses to inject some warm personal encouragement. All regulations are repelling if they are not seen in the light of their ultimate purpose. Paul, therefore, exalts the church and her gospel as worthy of all self-denial and sacrificial service.

## I. THE CUSTODIAN OF THE CHRISTIAN MYSTERY (3:14–16)

In verse 14, Paul expresses the hope that he may supplement his written instructions by his personal counsel. He is concerned supremely with the proper conduct of members of the church, which he calls the household of God. The church is the living family of the living God and as such cannot be a static institution, doting on its past traditions. Rather must it be a vital, aggressive, spiritual organism, assaulting all the deeply entrenched evils of earth in the name of the living God.

### 1. *The Transmission of the Truth*

Paul is looking beyond the local church at Ephesus to which Timothy was then ministering, calling the church "the pillar and ground [support or bulwark] of the truth." He is here referring to the people of Christ everywhere who serve as the guardians of the truth against those who would distort and thus destroy the true gospel.

49

Although truth is grounded in God and cannot finally be twisted nor distorted, yet the truth as transmitted through the church into history is always subject to the misunderstanding of men. Christians, therefore, must be constantly alert to guard against innovations which would sever the gospel from its eternal and historical foundations.

## 2. *An Early Christian Hymn*

Some expositors see in the rhythmic pattern of the sixteenth verse the remnants of one of the earliest Christian hymns. It may be translated, "confessedly great" or "great indeed we confess is the mystery of our religion." "Mystery" here means revealed truth, that which once was concealed but now stands openly revealed. The Christian church, through this hymn, stood up to sing or declare in public the greatness of its religion. Even as the pagan Ephesians sang "Great is Diana [Artemis] of the Ephesians" (Acts 19:28), this phrase seems to have been a common formula for confession of Christian faith.

In the Greek manuscripts the six rhythmic phrases are in the language of poetry. Translation into prose is difficult. Recognizing the difficulties, we undertake the following interpretation:

Paul's insistence that "God was manifest in the flesh" shows the primacy of the incarnation in the thought of the apostle. Our Lord's human nature and form were real.

"Justified [vindicated] in the Spirit" (3:16) is probably a reference to the fact that although our Lord lived in the flesh yet did he live above all transgression and sin. He conquered all temptation. Sinful men adjudged him guilty of blasphemy because he claimed to be the Son of God, and they put him to death; but God reversed the verdict and vindicated him through the power of the Holy Spirit, by raising him from the dead. Thus, Paul wrote in Romans 1:4 that Jesus is "declared to be the Son of God with power, according to the Spirit of holiness, by the resurrection from the dead" (ASV).

"Seen of angels" is probably a reference to the exaltation of Jesus as he is triumphant over the spirit world. Paul wrote in Philippians 2:9–10: "Wherefore God also hath highly exalted him, and given him a name which is above every name: that at the name of Jesus every knee should bow, of things in heaven, and things in earth, and things under the earth."

Paul speaks again most specifically of Christ's triumph in Colossians 2:15: "And having spoiled principalities and powers, he made a show of them openly, triumphing over them in it." The writer of Hebrews, in chapters 1 and 2, emphasizes the superiority of Christ to the angels.

It is possible that Paul could here (1 Tim. 3:16) be thinking of evil angels as the "principalities," "powers," "the world-rulers of this darkness," "the spiritual hosts of wickedness in the heavenly places" (Eph. 6:12 ASV). These powers were construed as being in league to crucify the Saviour. When he arose from the dead and ascended into heaven, he did so as the Conqueror and Lord of all angels.

"Preached among the nations" (ASV) emphasizes the universal scope of the proclamation of the gospel. "Believed on in the world" declares that this preaching has always been effective in the kindling of Christian faith.

In the light of the interpretation placed on the phrase "seen of angels," the concluding refrain, "received up in glory" seems redundant. This phrase may be regarded as typical of the poetic parallelism in Hebrew poetry. It speaks of the supremacy of Christ in heaven.

Remember that this letter is addressed to Timothy at Ephesus. There it was the custom to sing hymns of praise and adoration to Artemis of the Ephesians. Christians hearing such hymns would quite naturally sing hymns of adoration to Christ. By her pagan populace Ephesus was regarded as the "temple-keeper of the great Diana, and of the image which fell down from Jupiter" (Acts 19:35 ASV). Christians regarded the church in Ephesus as the custodian of a gospel which declared that its Lord had been exalted above all the earth in the glory of heaven.

## II. WARNINGS AGAINST HERESY (4:1-5)

Paul knew full well that the followers of Christ would be under constant temptation to depart from the faith. "In truth, the Spirit has expressly predicted such apostasy," says Paul. The New Testament takes into account that many persons have religious experiences which are too superficial to withstand the pressure of seducing spirits. Only those who have genuine saving faith can overcome the deceitful spirits which war against their souls.

It would seem that when Paul speaks of "the latter times" (4:1) he has in mind not so much a remote day in the distant future but the very day in which he was living. For Paul the latter days were even then upon the world. God had spoken his final word in Christ. Already the apostle was seeing men forsaking their religious faith and departing from Christ. Paul attributes this departure to the influence of heretical teachers who were inspired by demons. For him there was no middle ground. Either men were under the control of Christ or they were under the control of demons.

### 1. *The False Teachers*

Being under the control of demons, these teachers were liars. They played the role of believers yet actually were arch deceivers. They were hypocrites. Paul holds them fully responsible for their actions, despite their being under the control of demons. Many refuse today to accept the doctrine of a personal devil on the grounds that such a belief is a psychological gimmick which enables us to escape our personal responsibility for our wrongdoing by saying, "The devil compelled me!" This passage, however, makes it clear that these false teachers of demonic doctrines had consciences and were, therefore, responsible. They had, however, so long refused to observe the difference between right and wrong that now their consciences were so seared that they were chronic liars.

## 2. *Their False Attitude Toward Asceticism*

Paul is chiefly concerned with the heretical attitude toward the physical side of life. These false teachers were against the enjoyment of the physical side of marriage and the enjoyment of meats.

In the Greco-Roman world there were those who regarded everything physical as inherently evil. "Only the soul," they said, "is immortal. The body is subject to change and decay and will one day perish." Many of the Greeks held that salvation comes when the soul is delivered from the body. The most superior spiritual status could be achieved, they said, through austere renunciation of all fleshly desires. Abstinence from sex and from the eating of flesh was regarded as especially meritorious.

The Christian view, which resembles the Hebraic tradition, is that God is the Creator of all things. All things derive their goodness from God, the good Creator. "Every moving thing that liveth shall be food for you" (Gen. 9:3). The Christian view, however, supersedes the Levitical distinction between "clean" and "unclean" foods, insisting that there are no foods from which a Christian need abstain—except for reasons of health or influence.

Paul counsels neither ascetic denial nor unbridled liberty in the enjoyment of life's common pleasures. He lays down this principle: "You may freely and cheerfully enjoy everything for which you can sincerely thank God. On the other hand, you must uncompromisingly reject everything for which you cannot thank God" (1 Tim. 4:4–5). Everything for which man can truly thank God is good. The Christian is to enjoy life as God made it and not subject himself to unnatural restraints as though he could strengthen his soul thereby.

Paul insists, however, that while all things created by God are good, all things are not holy. They are made holy as they are dedicated to God for his purposes. They are "sanctified by the word of God and prayer" (4:5). "The word of God" is probably a reference specifically to the passage in Genesis 1:31: "And God saw everything that he had made, and, behold, it was very good."

False teachers often lure members of the church into sects which major on a type of asceticism which is utterly foreign to the life of the Man of Nazareth, who did not impose upon the shoulders of men impossible burdens that were grievous to be borne. Paul, therefore, appeals to the Christians to cling fast to the positive essentials of the Christian doctrine and not to become entangled with regulations which false teachers would use to pervert the faith.

## III. CHARACTERISTICS OF A GOOD MINISTER (4:6–10)

Four positive things Paul tells us must be true of a good minister of Jesus Christ.

### 1. *Instructing the Brotherhood*

He must, first of all, give clear instructions to the brotherhood, teaching them to discern between the positive essentials of the Christian faith and the innovations imposed by heretics. It is in the careful ministering to others that the servants of Christ are nourished in the words of faith and of good doctrine. Only through diligent study, through careful incorporation of the principles of the faith into his own life, and through laying the whole gospel before those whom he is given to serve, may the minister or any Christian leader nourish his own soul.

## 2. Refusing Myths and Speculations

The good minister, ordinarily being a man of broad knowledge, is often prone to be very charitable toward views contrary to his own. Especially is this true if he be a man of gentle and peaceable nature. He must be warned, therefore, against myths which often masquerade under the guise of religious truth. Timothy is thus warned to have nothing to do with "profane and old wives' fables [godless and silly myths]" (4:7). Doctrines which insist on abstinence from marriage and from certain foods are godless in that they have grown up in the foolish minds of men. Although they pretend to be religious, in reality they have nothing to do with the religion of Christ.

Many a Christian becomes obsessed with speculative schemes and prophetic patterns the pursuit of which he allows to become a hobby. He forces the Scriptures to coincide with his schemes and, often unknowingly, propagates a religion of fables and myths which are the products of his overheated imagination. Timothy, therefore, is warned against all religious nonsense. He is not to be lured into speculation, but must hold fast the faith which he has received from the apostle.

## 3. Exercising Self-discipline

Strong religion is the result of strong discipline and rigid training. Paul uses a word which normally meant to exert oneself in physical exercise when he wrote "exercise thyself rather unto godliness" (4:7), that is, put forth strong effort to discipline yourself in the way of godliness. Paul is saying that while bodily exercise is of limited value, godliness is of value in every way (4:8). That is to say, the training which one gives his soul will not only make life strong and pleasant and thus profit him in his earthly existence, but it will also carry over into the life to come and profit him eternally.

### 4. *Laboring and Trusting*

The Christian, therefore, is to toil, not as an athlete who strives for a wreath that perishes, but as one whose reward endures beyond this perishable realm. His trust is in the living God. His hope is secure, for the God who has given him life can continue to bestow it forever. Such assurance will warrant the most strenuous training and toil. The God in whom Paul was trusting is potentially the Saviour of all men; his saving grace is adequate for all who will believe; it is effective for all who do believe.

## IV. CHARACTER ABOVE CHRONOLOGY (4:11–16)

In this passage Paul gives some specific commands concerning the example of the pastor.

### 1. *The Pastor's Conduct*

How old Timothy actually was at the time of the writing of this epistle we cannot say. In that day the term youth was applied even to a full-grown man up to forty years of age. A pastor carries such heavy responsibilities in dealing with eternal verities that some in his congregation will always regard him as being too young. His only means of compensating for his youthfulness is by providing a superior moral and spiritual example for the believers. It is character, not chronology that counts with God. The young pastor— and, indeed, any young Christian worker—is to give no one grounds for despising his youth through default of character. The public life of every Timothy must be above reproach in that his speech and his conduct must coincide with his gospel. His private life must also call forth the esteem of his congregation as he cultivates love, faith, and purity.

## 2. *The Pastor's Use of the Scriptures*

There is no place for illiteracy in the Christian ministry. The apostle Paul makes it emphatically clear that men called of God to proclaim the unsearchable riches of Christ must be men of knowledge. The Christian religion has a written revelation, and only men who give themselves to the mastery of that revelation are qualified to serve as pastors of churches.

One of Paul's strongest admonitions to Timothy was, "Till I come, give attendance to reading" (4:13). This verse has been taken by very high authorities as a command to be careful in the public reading of the Scriptures. The preacher of Nehemiah's day stood "upon a pulpit of wood" and read the law of God distinctly and gave the meaning and caused the people to understand the reading (Neh. 8:4-8). This was our Lord's method, as was manifested when the book was delivered to him by the minister in the synagogue on the sabbath day (Luke 4:16-17).

We are told in the book of Acts that this custom in reading was practiced in that day (see Acts 13:15; 15:21). The Greek and Latin pattern also followed this method. We still have the expository lectures of Chrysostom and Augustine. We know also that Calvin stood in his pulpit of wood and read the Word of God distinctly and explained it until his congregation in Geneva understood.

On the other hand, certain scholars interpret this passage (4:13) to mean that Paul is not speaking so much of Timothy's pulpit ministry as of his personal and private devotional attention to the Bible. They contend that Paul is saying, in effect:

"Timothy, read distinctly and preach convincingly in your pulpit. Yet, above all else, let the Word of God dwell richly in yourself. Even though you have learned the holy Scriptures as a child, you must not allow a day to pass in which you do not call them to mind in your reading and meditation. Take heed unto thyself. You must give attention to your doctrine, but even more to your deportment. Your primary duty as a pastor is not to set yourself up as a pattern to your people but to strive so to live that they will see that you are a living example of your message."

The pastor who constantly takes heed to himself in his conversation and manner of living, in preaching better every Sunday, in discharging all the endless duties of his pastorate, in holding his peace in controversy, and in a life of secret faith and prayer—such a pastor, God will surely honor and his congregation will most certainly emulate.

"Till I come" is probably Paul's way of assuring Timothy that, in the apostle's absence, Timothy was in full charge of the church at Ephesus and was held fully responsible for the nurture of the souls given into his care. The three phases of pastoral ministry mentioned are reading, exhortation, and teaching (4:13 ASV). All of these presuppose a period of study and training. "Reading" means the public reading aloud of the Scriptures. "Exhortation" is that preaching of the Scriptures which appeals to the moral sense and which motivates the congregation to put the Scriptures into practice. "Teaching" is the informing of the Christian intellect of the basic principles of the Christian faith.

### 3. *The Exercise of the Pastor's Gift*

God calls no man to a task without giving him at the same time the ability to perform it. This passage insists that Timothy had the gift to preach and teach, which was given of God through the prophetic utterance which constituted his call and which was acknowledged in Timothy's ordination when the hands of the presbytery were placed upon him. Timothy is warned not to neglect this gift, for the most important part of his ministry is not in his reception of the gift but in his faithful use of it for the purpose for which it was bestowed.

The discipline of the minister includes far more than secluded study. Much of what the servant of Christ knows must be learned amid the performance of the manifold duties enjoined upon him. The King James translation, "Meditate upon these things" (4:15) is not, therefore, the best translation. The word actually means "practice these things," "exercise thyself in" or "be diligent in." The work of the good pastor includes public reading of the Scriptures, preaching, and teaching. He is to devote himself to this threefold ministry. As Moffatt translates it, "Let them absorb you."

Maturity in the ministry does not come through a miracle. It comes only through steady, disciplined study and faithful practice of the Christian precepts. Such study and practice produce spiritual maturity even in youthful leaders, a maturity which no man can justifiably despise.

The good servant of Christ must have a dual concern: (1) He must be concerned for his own spiritual well-being, since he is the channel through which the gospel must pass to others. The channel must, therefore, be straight. (2) He must be equally concerned with the spiritual well-being of those whom God has given him to love.

If a pastor, or any Christian leader is concerned only with his own spiritual well-being, he may find himself losing his life through trying to save it.

## SUGGESTIONS FOR STUDY AND DISCUSSION

1. Let the class suggest stanzas of well-known hymns which may correspond with statements in 1 Timothy 3:16.
2. Discuss the Greek attitude toward the physical side of life as it contrasts with the Christian viewpoint.
3. List the four positive things Paul says must be true of a good minister of Jesus Christ (1 Tim. 4:6–10).
4. Discuss Paul's specific commands concerning the example of the pastor.

# CHAPTER 5

I. A PASTOR'S ATTITUDE TOWARD ELDERS (5:1–2)

II. THE CHURCH'S TREATMENT OF WIDOWS (5:3–16)

   1. Actual Dependency
   2. Rigid Regulations
   3. The Younger Widows

III. HOW TO TREAT CHURCH OFFICIALS (5:17–25)

   1. Adequate Financial Compensation
   2. Care for the Pastor's Reputation
   3. A Charge to the Pastor

IV. DUTIES OF CHRISTIAN SLAVES (6:1–2$b$)

   1. The Indirect Attack on Slavery
   2. The Word of God Changing Social Customs

V. THE NECESSITY OF SOUND TEACHING (6:2$c$–5)

VI. CHRISTIAN CONTENTMENT (6:6–10)

   1. The Importance of Contentment
   2. The Meaning of Contentment
   3. Abiding Treasures
   4. The Moral Issues Involved

# 5

# *How Various Church Groups Should Be Treated*

## I. A Pastor's Attitude Toward Elders (5:1-2)

Since a Christian church is a family, the pastor must respect the older members of the congregation as he respects his own father. He must not fall prey to the constant temptation which besets each new generation to despise the generation that has gone before. He must not use his pulpit as a secure fortress from which to hurl harsh and violent reproof against the older, more conservative members of his congregation, as if his is the only generation which has actually known the wisdom of God. Few things are more pathetic in a church than the encounter which often rages between youth and age.

It is quite natural for each new generation to be impatient with all that went before. It is also quite natural for each generation as it grows older to become strongly critical of that which follows. But the church is the home of the supernatural grace of God where this impatience and hypercritical attitude must be subdued.

The church recognizes the need of both youth and age. Youth is needed to give new enthusiasm to a weary world and to supply bright, clear eyes with which to examine truths that have lost their luster because of their familiarity. Youth must keep the spirit of sturdy valor and high adventure in our world. But age is also needed to counterbalance youth's frothy enthusiasm with the stability that comes only through experience.

Elders in the church are to be entreated with the kindly spirit one would have toward his own father. The word translated "intreat" (5:1) actually embraces the ideas of exhortation, admonition, and comfort. Paul is insisting that the pastor must not rule his congregation with pompous harshness but with the affection he would show toward his own family, regarding the older members as mothers and fathers in Christ and the younger members as brothers and sisters in Christ. There is a proper word of caution at the close of the second verse, calling the pastor to remember that his affection for the younger women must be within the bounds of perfect propriety and purity.

## II. THE CHURCH'S TREATMENT OF WIDOWS (5:3–16)

Because so many demands were made upon the treasury of the early church, the apostle cautions against lack of wisdom in the disbursement of the church's charity funds.

### 1. *Actual Dependency*

Widows must be properly cared for with genuine compassion, but they must be in real need, and must not be pampered. To "honor," in Paul's mind, meant to respect and support (5:3). By "widows indeed" he means, not simply women who had lost their husbands, but those who had lost all kinsfolk who would have been obligated by family ties to provide for them. Goodspeed translates this passage, "Look after widows who are really dependent." [1]

The "real widow" must not only be without children or grandchildren who could support her, but she must give herself faithfully to supplications and prayers night and day. Inasmuch as she is "desolate" (all alone) and "trusteth [solely] in God" and is faithful in her service for him, she has a right to be supported by the people of God, the church

(5:5). Furthermore, these widows must not be under sixty years of age (5:9). When we remember that only one hundred years ago the average life span was forty years, we can imagine how few widows in the early church would have met the age requirement. The widow must have been the wife of one husband.

## 2. *Rigid Regulations*

But Paul does not stop there; he lays down even more rigid regulations (5:10). She must have had a reputation for good works, must have reared children, and shown hospitality to strangers. Christianity was a religion on the move, therefore, every Christian was obligated to be hospitable to every other Christian. The "real widow" must "have washed the saints' feet." She must not feel herself above the most common task. She must be willing to do even the work of a slave. She must also have cared for the sick and the poor. Her life, in brief, must have been full of every kind of good work.

These rigid regulations manifest that the church, while genuinely concerned for relieving real need, was not to pamper anyone and contribute to his degeneration through an unregulated dole system. Only widows who met the foregoing requirements were "enrolled" (5:9 ASV). The word "enrolled" may denote an official order of workers to which "real widows" were admitted. If so, the early church apparently kept records of these full-time workers.

The necessity of the church's caring for destitute widows had a moral as well as a material basis. If the needy women were not cared for, they might be tempted to turn to worldly or sinful pursuits in an effort to gain a livelihood. Verse 6 suggests this. The honor of the church was, therefore, at stake. These widows should be assisted in retaining their honor that they might not be dead to the Christian life and bring reproach upon the church.

Individual members of the church are sternly warned against refusing support to their own kinsfolk (5:8). If any able member of the church refuses to support a kinsman, thus allowing him to become a burden on the church, he is guilty of denying the faith "and is worse than an infidel," or unbeliever. That is to say, he has placed the financial gain derived from the church's support of his kinsman above his religious faith. He is worse than an infidel, for the infidel at least remains outside of the church, while the selfish kinsman remains inside for the purpose of exploiting the church.

### 3. The Younger Widows

In the case of widows who were under sixty years of age, Paul has clear command. The word translated "I will" (5:14) means "I command." This command includes three specific requirements: They must marry, bear children, and care for their households. They should not be "enrolled" (5:9 ASV). All of this Paul commands that the outside world might not reproach the church.

Young widows would be more prone to allow their visiting from house to house in the name of the church to become an occasion for becoming idlers, gossips, and busybodies, peddling malicious gossip. Older widows would have adequately demonstrated that they were above dissipating their religious service in this manner. Paul had in mind, apparently, some specific instances where younger widows had brought scandal into the church by their misconduct and had played into the hands of Satan, the adversary of the church (5:15).

### III. How to Treat Church Officials (5:17–25)

Paul was a craftsman who labored with his hands in the making of tents that he might not be a burden to the early Christian churches. Paul's example is often cited by uninformed Christians as proof that the pastors of churches today should make their living through employment in secular work.

## 1. *Adequate Financial Compensation*

It should be remembered, however, that Paul was an establisher of churches, not a pastor of strong, established institutions. Paul teaches explicitly that those who preach and teach in churches are entitled not only to the prestige and honor of their positions, but also to adequate financial compensation (5:18). He argues here not only for a paid ministry, but for an adequately paid ministry.

Those pastors who were good administrators were, in the eyes of Paul, entitled to double honor (5:17). That "double honor" actually means double pay is clearly shown in the context. Those who were good administrators and who, in addition, preached and taught were entitled to additional compensation. The tone of the passage seems to imply that this was the practice.

Yet, even as is still true, there were those in that distant day who felt that a preacher should not receive compensation for his work. Paul, therefore, found it necessary to insist that to give financial compensation was just and that the members of the church should not begrudge an adequate salary for their pastor, nor should they deliberately keep his salary as low as possible. (Compare Matt. 10:10; Luke 10:7; 1 Cor. 9:3–9; 2 Tim. 2:6.)

A good minister of Christ should be provided with the means for meeting his obligations promptly, that the church might not be despised by unbelievers. The pastor who, with a clear vision of the spiritual principles involved, leads a congregation to supply him with the means to educate his children and to provide a measure of security for the years when he can no longer labor is not, therefore, dishonoring Christ.

Church members may crush the heart out of a man of God, or other member of the church staff, not primarily because they do not insist on adequate compensation but because their failure to insist on such betokens a dearth of affection which is the very manna of heaven upon which the Christian worker must feed.

To bolster his argument for adequate compensation for ministers, Paul reaches back into the Old Testament for one quotation: "Thou shalt not muzzle the ox when he treadeth out the corn" (Deut. 25:4). To refuse compensation to a pastor is like placing an ox in the midst of an abundance of potential food and compelling him to do the work which makes the food useful to man, while he is denied the right to partake of the food himself. Paul further reinforces his argument by recalling the statement of Jesus, "The labourer is worthy of his hire" (Luke 10:7). Moffatt translates this, "A workman deserves his wages." Paul thus based his authority on the Word of God that was available in his day. Therefore, his word must not be taken as an irrelevant, secondary opinion.

## 2. Care for the Pastor's Reputation

Not only must the members guard the honor of the church by adequately caring for the pastor, they must also guard the reputation of the pastor against loose, irresponsible criticism. They must realize that men in prominent positions in the church are the constant targets of malicious criticism. Since the most ancient method of bolstering one's own prestige is by criticising the most important person one knows, Paul warns the congregation to take this fact into full account in judging any criticism levied against the pastor.

The fellowship of love between the pastor and his people should be so strong that the pastor may be able to rest his case in the hands of his congregation with the perfect assurance that they will fight his battles for him against those who would destroy the church by, first of all, destroying the pastor's reputation. In the light of this fact, Paul forbids a church to even bring a minister to trial unless the charges against him can be justified by two or three witnesses.

On the other hand, because there are congregations whose affection for the pastor is so strong that they may overlook his moral failures, Paul gives orders that when guilt is established the pastor must be publicly reprimanded (5:20). Perhaps the better translation is, "those who persist in sin." The implication is that a pastor's guilt has been established and he has been privately reprimanded, yet he continues in wrongdoing. He must, therefore, be severely handled. His public rebuke will restrain others from following his moral failure.

### 3. *A Charge to the Pastor*

Timothy is solemnly charged before the court of heaven, God, the Lord Jesus Christ, and the elect angels which surround the throne of God, to observe Paul's instructions in dealing with offenders (5:21). Partiality must not be shown, for ultimately all must stand before the judgment, when God, Christ, and the elect angels will be present and no evil men can be shielded and no innocent man condemned.

Because disciplining workers in the church is so exceedingly difficult, great caution must be observed in selecting them (5:22). By partaking in the selection of improper persons, Timothy would be actually a partaker of their sins against the church. His own purity, therefore, is bound up in the careful selection of those who serve as leaders in the church.

A very practical and personal word is spoken to Timothy in verse 23. It is apparent that the Gnostic asceticism was influencing him. Wine was used medicinally in Timothy's day. But his scruples apparently had caused him to refrain not only from using it as a beverage but also from taking it as a medicine.

It is also very probable that the heresy was already at work in Ephesus that healing must be by spiritual means only and all medicines must be refused. Paul, therefore, repudiates both the unreasonable asceticism and the preposterous position of the faith healers by expressly encouraging Timothy, "Use a little wine for thy stomach's sake and thine often infirmities" (5:23).

Paul closes the chapter (vv. 24–25) by assuring Timothy that, while it is not always easy to distinguish between good and evil, yet there is an eternal distinction between them, and one day this distinction will be clearly revealed.

## IV. Duties of Christian Slaves (6:1–2b)

Many of the members of the early church were slaves. The question arises, Why does Paul seem to countenance slavery? It must be remembered that a direct attack upon the practice would have caused misunderstanding in the church and would probably have led to an ineffectual, open rebellion against a deeply entrenched institution, which would, no doubt, have resulted in widespread suffering.

### 1. The Indirect Attack on Slavery

Paul chose to attack the institution of slavery indirectly. He knew that a virile Christian gospel, practiced both by masters and slaves, would inevitably lead to the pulling down of the strongholds of slavery. While there are occasions when positive, direct action against social evils is demanded on the part of Christians, there are other times when it is better to allow the gospel leaven to work gradually. Paul, therefore, does not counsel open rebellion on the part of the slaves. Instead he urges them to "count their own masters worthy of all honour" (6:1).

The apostle frankly acknowledges the evil involved in slavery, for he describes it as being "under the yoke." He, however, in this passage is concerned primarily with one matter, not the comfort of the Christian slave, but that the "name of God and his doctrine be not blasphemed." Paul could foresee a great blasphemy against the Christian gospel as a result of the social upheaval which might follow the forceful abolishing of slavery. The greater progress of the gospel would be made within the existing social order, therefore, the apostle points out that the duty of the Christian slave is to offer his master his complete respect.

## 2. The Word of God Changing Social Customs

It seems to be a common fault among reformers to be very zealous and valiant in the initial efforts to bring about a reformation and then to lose interest in the tedious tasks that must be patiently performed in carrying through to completion. The most enduring reformation comes through sustained patient devotion to the task.

The lesson is the same as that which came to Elijah on Mount Horeb after his zealous effort at reform on Mount Carmel. The wind, the earthquake, and the fire may be used of God to gain man's attention; the spectacular may break through the barriers of man's complacency. But the power of God to bring about social reforms works most surely in the "still small voice" of a sustained teaching program.

A. N. Whitehead shows how the destruction of the institution of slavery in the British Empire came about. He said in effect: It was the Methodist revival of the eighteenth century which "produced the final effective force which hereafter made slavery impossible among progressive races." True, "the Methodist preachers aimed at saving men's souls in the next world." But "they made the conception of the brotherhood of man and of the importance of men, a vivid reality." Their virile preaching undermined the institution of slavery in the British Empire and prepared the way for the final decisive blow dealt by the abolitionists under Wilberforce.[2]

Both slaves and masters may settle their problems only in the spirit of Christian brotherhood. If a Christian slave had a Christian master, he should be most grateful for his good fortune. A slave might easily be tempted to take advantage of a Christian master and become insolent and indolent. To avoid this temptation, the slave must remember that the one who benefits from his toil is a beloved brother; he should, therefore, toil all the better. Slaves must remember that, while in the church men are brothers, these same men live out their lives in a social order which is not Christian. The Christian ideal creates a tension between good and evil, in the discomfort of which tension Christians must live out their lives.

## V. The Necessity of Sound Teaching (6:2c–5)

The early Christian church encountered a world which was continually in search of new religious ideas. Luke tells us that the Athenians "spent their time in nothing else, but either to tell, or to hear some new thing" (Acts 17:21). Timothy had, therefore, to be cautioned against giving ground before novel teachings and new fads which continually threatened to distort the true Christian message. Only the teachings which Paul had received from Christ and had passed on to Timothy were to be considered as authoritative in the early church.

In verse 3 Paul reprimands those teachers whose pride and eagerness for personal display permit them to substitute controversial questions for the simple truth about the Saviour. Moffatt translates verse 3: "Anyone who teaches novelties and refuses to fall in with the sound words of our Lord Jesus Christ and the doctrine that tallies with godliness, is a conceited, ignorant creature."

Strife over words and petty religious debate never leads to the truth but to malicious suspicions about those who differ from us. Where there is envy and strife, stronger barriers arise through which the truth of God cannot penetrate. When men of corrupt minds give themselves to perverse disputings about religion, they miss the truth because they identify gain with godliness or they think of religion as a means of gain.

"Men who are so puffed up with conceit that they will not submit to the revelation of God in Christ," says Paul, in effect, "have a morbid craving to the point of being so morally and spiritually sick that they cannot refrain from speculative debates about religious words to justify themselves. In their frenzied debating they deviate so far from the truth of the gospel that religion comes to mean nothing to them but a way of making money." This warning could be a reference to certain religious hucksters who were willing to fan a community into flaming controversy to draw interest and attendance, take up their offerings, then depart, leaving the Christians of the community locked in an encounter which might damage the fellowship of the churches for years.

The warning regarding false teachers is no incidental comment in Paul's writing. It is significant that a large percentage of the material in 1 and 2 Timothy deals with the teaching ministry of the church. Indeed many Bible students would select the statement in 1 Timothy 4:16, "Take heed unto thyself, and unto the doctrine [teaching]" as the key verse for both epistles.

## VI. CHRISTIAN CONTENTMENT (6:6–10)

Paul, no doubt, had often found himself comparing his lot with the most comfortable circumstances in which the Jewish rabbis lived out their lives. Paul had received the same training as they. He had been educated under Gamaliel and had been a worthy student. He had chosen to walk the austere road of self-denial with the Saviour. He said, on one occasion, "I have learned, in whatsoever state I am, therewith to be content" (Phil. 4:11). This attitude was something Paul had to learn, as every servant of Christ must learn it.

## 1. *The Importance of Contentment*

It is doubtful if a Christian worker can get very far in his service to Christ and humanity if he ever becomes obsessed with the desire to improve his material well-being. It is true that the New Testament teaches that "they which preach the gospel should live of the gospel" (1 Cor. 9:14), yet this situation is something that only the congregation can bring to pass.

"The role of the pastor," says Paul, "is to remember that godliness with contentment is great gain" (6:6). He does not say that godliness is great gain, for there are many godly people who are not content. We are ever wanting more and are ever unmindful of the blessings we have until they are taken from us.

Suppose that any one of us were suddenly stricken with some incurable disease, leukemia, paralysis, or muscular dystrophy? Then how suddenly all of his other concerns would vanish into oblivion and his only prayer would be, "O Lord, give me back my health that I may again be with my friends in the work of thy kingdom!"

## 2. *The Meaning of Contentment*

Contentment does not mean self-satisfaction, for if one is ever satisfied with himself he begins to degenerate. If one feels that he has attained the higher standards of God in Christ Jesus, he merely manifests that he has become spiritually blind and has so lowered those standards and accommodated them to his own meager pattern of living that he no longer distinguishes between God's standards and his own. It is the function of the gospel to make the conscience sensitive and to disturb men in their imperfections until they shall be willing to be lifted out of them.

Contentment, on the other hand, has to do with the externalities of life. It is the cure for coveteousness, which is idolatry. The gain toward which a Christian pastor and his congregation must, therefore, strive is to be defined in spiritual terms, godliness with contentment. The true gain which religion affords is never primarily material. It may be true that physical and material well-being are the by-products of a proper relationship with God and fellow man. Nevertheless, the emphasis of this passage is upon the truth that the primary gain bestowed by true religion is in terms of godly living, which gives a man a sense of adequacy that produces contentment. He is then trusting not in the abundance of things which he possesses but in the grace of God which is able to make him adequate to supply his own needs.

## 3. *Abiding Treasures*

Wealth is not essential to man's ultimate well-being. "He did not have it," says Paul, "before he came into this world, nor will he have it in the world to come." The abiding treasures must, therefore, be seen in terms of Christlikeness. Whatever else we may have in eternity, of this we may be most certain, we shall have ourselves there. The goal toward which we should strive in life, should, therefore, be in terms of those qualities of soul which make us Christlike. "For we brought nothing into this world, and it is certain we can carry nothing out" (6:7). Mere wealth is not ultimately essential to the well-being of the soul; why then should we center all of life around its accumulation or regard it as an end in itself? It is far, far better to major on cultivating the enlargement of the soul that we may ultimately receive the fullness of the blessings of Christ.

In verse 8, Paul is following the explicit counsel of our Lord. "Provide neither gold, nor silver, nor brass in your purses, nor scrip for your journey, neither two coats neither shoes, nor yet staves, for the workman is worthy of his meat" (Matt. 10:9–10). "Take no thought for your life, what ye shall eat, or what ye shall drink; nor yet for your body, what ye shall put on. Is not the life more than meat, and the body than raiment?" (Matt. 6:25). Paul's word is, "Having food and raiment [which includes shelter] let us be therewith content" (6:8).

### 4. *The Moral Issues Involved*

The apostle does not condemn the possession of wealth as such. The great moral questions must gather around how one makes his money, how he uses it, and to whom the owner considers himself accountable for its use. Paul declares that those who are subject to being ensnared into the foolish and hurtful lusts which plunge men into destruction are not necessarily those who have wealth but those who desire to have it.

The greed for gold often drags men down to destruction. Addressing the Harvard Chapel, Francis G. Peabody related Ruskin's story of a man who attempted to swim to safety from a wrecked ship, with a belt containing two hundred pounds in gold tied about his waist. He could not leave the gold behind, nor could he make it to shore with his gold. They were inseparable. With it he went down. Ruskin asked this question, "As he was sinking, had he the gold or had the gold him?" [3]

A popular proverb of Paul's day, "For the love of money is the root of all evil," (6:10) is here incorporated into the Scriptures. "All evil" no doubt means that the heart that is set on money will stoop to any ruthless method or misdeed to get it. This represents for a Christian a deserting of the Redeemer, a repudiation of his principles, and a manifestation that one has departed from an enduring, obedient faith and is, therefore, in unspeakable pangs of spiritual anguish.

## SUGGESTIONS FOR STUDY AND DISCUSSION

1. Compare the benevolent program of your church with that endorsed by Paul for the early churches.
2. Let the class discuss the teachings in 1 Timothy regarding the financial care of pastors.
3. Place on the chalkboard a list of ways in which a congregation may enlarge and enhance the pastor's ministry.
4. How may we apply Paul's strategy in pulling down the strongholds of the institution of slavery to our modern approaches to social problems? How should we decide when the gradual approach is right and when to engage in open attack against some moral or social evil?
5. Let the class discuss what Paul's position on Christian contentment in 1 Timothy 6:4-10 has to say to the modern clash between labor and management.

---

[1] Edgar J. Goodspeed, *The Goodspeed Parallel New Testament* (Chicago: The University of Chicago Press, 1943), p. 485. Used by permission.

[2] Whitehead, *Adventures of Ideas* (New York: The Macmillan Co., 1933), pp. 27-28 *passim.* Used by permission of publisher.

[3] Francis G. Peabody, *Mornings in the College Chapel* (2d series; Boston: Houghton Mifflin Co., 1907), p. 2.

# CHAPTER 6

I.  THE CHRISTIAN'S WARFARE (6:11–16)

1.  An Aggressive Warfare
2.  A Profound Charge
3.  An Inspiring Example

II.  THE CONDUCT OF RICH CHRISTIANS (6:17–19)

1.  The Christian Attitude Toward Wealth
2.  Earning Spiritual Dividends

III.  THE FINAL CALL TO FAITHFULNESS (6:20–21)

1.  Approaches to Knowledge
2.  Speculation Contrasted with Revealed Truth
3.  Conclusion of the Letter

# 6

# *Final Call to Faithfulness*

## I. The Christian's Warfare (6:11-16)

"Transcending every other consideration," says Paul, "Timothy, as a Christian pastor, must remember that he is a man of God." He has been called to a high position of leadership. His example will be a most decisive factor in molding the conduct of his congregation. He rests under the solemn obligation to act as "a man of God."

It should be remembered that the term "man of God" never occurs in the plural in the New Testament. It is a term setting apart from the congregation the man who has a special calling to the ministry. Special endowments involve special responsibilities before God.

While strict exegesis requires that we keep in mind that Timothy was a pastor, it is also true that the principles set forth in this chapter, and indeed throughout most of the epistle, have a comprehensive application to all Christian workers, whether they are employed in church-related vocations or serve as volunteers.

### 1. An Aggressive Warfare

Timothy must exercise himself aggressively against the temptations which confronted him. He must "flee" from covetousness and all the evils into which covetousness would attempt to plunge him. Furthermore, he must positively follow after the foremost Christian virtues. He was under a vow to be loyal to the gospel which he preached,

77

which includes righteousness, godliness, faith, love, patience, and gentleness.

The Christian's responsibility to be aggressive in his work is emphasized in his call to "fight the good fight of faith" (6:12). The New Testament abounds in athletic metaphors which depict the Christian's conflict with evil. The Christian must make certain that he is fighting on the right side, "the good fight." In so doing, he will be laying hold even in the present on eternal life. Paul, in this passage, seems to think of eternal life as that quality of life which begins the moment one puts his faith in the Saviour. The high fulfilment of this life, however, comes at the end of the Christian warfare. To this life eternal, Timothy had been called. He responded to this call through his profession of Christ as Lord before both those witnesses who scoffed as he turned away from them and those who rejoiced as he entered the fellowship of the redeemed.

## 2. A Profound Charge

It would be difficult to imagine a more solemn and profound charge than that which Paul issues to Timothy as he calls him to keep the commandment to "fight the good fight of faith, lay hold on eternal life." This charge is given in the sight of God, "who alone hath immortality" (6:16). Only the immortal can give life eternal. Our God dwells in light unapproachable and cannot be seen by any human effort. If God is seen, he must reveal himself, and no man can approach God unless he be drawn by the Spirit of God. He alone is Sovereign in the universe. He is "King of kings and Lord of lords" (6:15). Before him then, Timothy is charged to keep this commandment.

## 3. An Inspiring Example

Moreover, Timothy is charged "before Christ Jesus, who before Pontius Pilate witnessed a good confession" (6:13).

Here Paul is calling Timothy to remember the consistency of the witness of Christ with the action of Christ. Before Pontius Pilate he bore his witness and then sealed it with his death. Christ's death, in truth, became his chief witness. He confessed before the high priest who asked him, "Art thou the Christ, the Son of the Blessed? And Jesus said, I am" (Mark 14:61–62). "The high priest rent his clothes and saith, What need we any further witnesses? Ye have heard the blasphemy" (Mark 14:63–64). The mob declared Jesus to be guilty of death.

Before Pontius Pilate, Jesus maintained his silence (Matt. 27:13–14; Mark 15:4–5), except for his answer to Pilate's one question (Mark 15:2). It seems that he sensed the futility of argument. He would go to his death on the grounds of his confession before Caiaphas that he was the Christ, the Son of the blessed. In the inspiration of Christ's own witness of a good confession, Timothy was to keep the commandment unstained and free from reproach until he should stand before Christ to be judged at his appearing.

## II. THE CONDUCT OF RICH CHRISTIANS (6:17–19)

Many writers are shocked by the abrupt transition from the high spiritual doxology to a straightforward word to the "rich in this world" (6:17). From a literary point of view, perhaps this epistle would be better balanced if it concluded with verse 16. Paul, however, had little time to be concerned with literary merit. His purpose was altogether practical. He knew full well how tremendously significant material wealth is in the spiritual lives of men.

### 1. *The Christian Attitude Toward Wealth*

Money in the long ago, even as today, was not merely money. It was wholesome food to eat and warm clothes and shelter for the children. It represented the ability to care for aging parents who could no longer care for themselves.

It was the ability to provide books and music and good teachers for children. It was the ability to help others in distress. It was the prospect of an old age free from haunting fear and anxiety. Just because there are many things that money cannot buy, the New Testament never closes its eyes to the things that money can buy. Anyone who has ever visited a slum knows what a horrible effect the lack of money has upon the moral and spiritual lives of its inhabitants.

The Christian church must remember the positive words of the Master and of the apostles concerning the high spiritual uses of our material substance. Christian pastors are unforgivably dilatory if they do not assist the wealthy members of their congregations to use their money to advance the kingdom.

Earthly riches must be regarded by the Christian as having only one purpose. They represent the potential which one has for gaining abiding riches. When Paul speaks of "them that are rich in this world," he means "in the present age." This is the apostle's way of emphasizing the ephemeral nature of all material wealth. Since this age is constantly passing away, all that by nature belongs to it will vanish.

The Christian man of wealth must not allow his wealth to make him haughty nor must he trust in his riches for his eternal well-being. His only ground of confidence must be in the living God who abides though all else vanishes. The Christian must look above his wealth and put his trust in the God who gave him everything which he enjoys. There is nothing wrong with a man's enjoying his wealth. In truth, it is given to him by a gracious God to enjoy. No man, however, can truly enjoy wealth who is more devoted to wealth (to the acquiring of it and the selfish use of it) than he is to God. God is the true fountain of abiding joy.

"In thy presence is fulness of joy; at thy right hand there are pleasures for evermore" (Psalm 16:11).

## 2. *Earning Spiritual Dividends*

The highest use of wealth is in the acknowledgement that God has given it that, through it, we may earn larger spiritual dividends. It affords us opportunities to be rich in good works. Money can be used to relieve the distressed, to feed the starving, to alleviate pain and provide medical care and, best of all, it can provide for the proclamation of the gospel of God's manifold love and redeeming grace. The Christian who has allowed the grace of God to take vital hold on his heart is thereby made gracious. He is liberal and generous and ready to distribute his wealth for the glory of God and the uplift of humanity. He shares the convictions of the poet, Whittier, whose words have challenged many to express Christian love in action:

> O brother man, fold to thy heart thy brother!
> Where pity dwells, the peace of God is there;
> To worship rightly is to love each other,
> Each smile a hymn, each kindly deed a prayer.
>
> Follow with rev'rent steps the great example
> Of Him whose holy work was doing good;
> So shall the wide earth seem our Father's temple,
> Each loving life a psalm of gratitude.
>
> JOHN G. WHITTIER

By practicing good deeds and by being liberal and generous, Christians will be "laying up in store [treasuring up] for themselves a good foundation" (6:19). The Christian whose life is outgoing to others in need is building his house of life on a rock, as the Master has taught (Matt. 7:24). In the world to come, the Christian who has used his money aright will know life as a great loving God intended it to be.

## III. The Final Call to Faithfulness (6:20–21)

The apostle Paul's supreme concern for Timothy was that he guard carefully the greatest of all treasures, the Christian gospel. He must make certain that it be passed on in its purity and that it not be perverted nor distorted by the "profane babblings and oppositions of the knowledge which is falsely so called" (6:20 ASV).

### 1. *Approaches to Knowledge*

There are two ordinary approaches to religious knowledge. There is the approach of science, which insists that knowledge must be the result of man's quest through the laboratory and through his logic; truth must be something which he can demonstrate for himself. Then there is the reverent approach which contends that knowledge in the ultimate sense must be divinely disclosed, must be revealed from above and made known to man not as though he were only an intellect but as a total personality.

God must disclose himself to man through a personal encounter with man. The Divine thus makes himself known by his impact upon the total personality of man. God addresses man's reason by saying to him that which may be above his reason and beyond his immediate comprehension but which is never against his reason. God addresses man's will by calling for the cessation of his moral rebellion against God and his surrender to the divine purposes; God addresses man's emotions by confronting him with a love which the world cannot give and cannot take away and thus eliciting from him a love which is deathless. By faithful, trusting obedience man thus comes to know God first in a moment of conversion; he goes on to increase in knowledge that involves reason, emotion, and volition, as he lives in the fellowship of God through faith in Christ.

## 2. *Speculation Contrasted with Revealed Truth*

"Contrasted with such a knowledge of God, all other knowledge," says Paul, "is godless chatter which contradicts the very possibility of knowledge of God which a Christian contends that he possesses." There have always been those religious syncretists who contend that the pathway to religious certainty is to take the mass of religious beliefs discovered by men and reduce them to their lowest common denominator. Over against this point of view, the Christian affirms that you do not get to the truth by multiplying error and reducing it to a level upon which all human wisdom can agree.

Truth on the highest plane is made real to us not through speculation but in the life of him who loved as never man loved, lived as never man lived, died as never man died, and broke the bonds of death to demonstrate that living Truth crushed to earth will surely rise again in person of the living Son of God. This is the only kind of truth that can transform and remake life. There is no redemptive power in an abstract idea, but truth incarnate in the life of Jesus of Nazareth has been and is remaking life every moment.

The knowledge which the apostle extols is "the knowledge of the truth." He uses different terms to designate the kind of knowledge which was proclaimed by the Gnostics—a knowledge which man creates for himself—and "the knowledge of the truth" which only God discloses through his Son. Those who think of religion merely as the product of the human intellect have "erred concerning the faith" (6:21).

## 3. *Conclusion of the Letter*

Only the grace of God, which caused him to take the initiative in coming to men whose intelligence was twisted and depraved by open rebellion against God, could reconcile such men to God and sustain them in the true fellowship of God and guard them against false teachers.

It was the grace of God which caused God to take the initiative and to break down the barriers which the twisted minds, depraved emotions, and enslaved wills of men had erected between themselves and God. It is now only the grace of God which can sustain the souls of men and guard them from error. Paul, therefore, concludes his letter with the prayer, "Grace be with you."

The inscription given in the King James Version as a footnote at the end of the epistles has raised some questions about the place of writing and the recipient of the epistle. However, this footnote is not on all the old manuscripts. It was certainly not written by Paul. It must not, therefore, be considered as disproving the conclusions which are discussed in the introduction to this textbook.

## SUGGESTIONS FOR STUDY AND DISCUSSION

1. List the suggestions which Paul made to rich Christians in 1 Timothy 6:17–19.
2. Contrast the two ordinary approaches to knowledge discussed in this chapter.

# PART TWO

# 2 TIMOTHY

# CHAPTER 7

I. THE SALUTATION (1:1–2)
    1. The Will of God
    2. Concern for Timothy

II. GRATITUDE FOR TIMOTHY'S SERVICE (1:3–7)
    1. Timothy's Religious Heritage
    2. Use of Spiritual Gifts
    3. God-given Courage

III. SUFFERING FOR THE GOSPEL (1:8–14)
    1. A Special Blessing
    2. The Holy Calling
    3. Light on Life and Immortality
    4. Confidence in Christ

IV. PAUL'S PERSONAL FRIENDSHIPS (1:15–18)
    1. The Desertion of Some Former Friends
    2. The Kindness of Onesiphorus

# 7

# *Gratitude for Timothy's Ministry*

BOTH OF Paul's letters to Timothy deal with the ministry of the servant of Christ in the church. A congregation is exceedingly blessed when she has a good minister of Jesus Christ as her undershepherd. It is the solemn responsibility of every church member to seek honestly to understand precisely what the definite work of the pastor is and carefully to guard him from that which would distract him from his heaven-appointed mission.

## I. THE SALUTATION (1:1–2)

This second letter to Timothy begins with the usual salutation, naming the writer and the recipient, then giving words of benediction.

### 1. *The Will of God*

The most stabilizing factor in the ministry of Paul was the assurance that he was in the ministry not primarily by his own choosing but by "the will of God" (1:1). The Damascus road experience in which it was said of Saul, "It is hard for thee to kick against the pricks" (Acts 9:5), portrays strong rebellion at first against the call of God. Nothing but the overpowering conviction that it was the will of God for his life could have made Paul a minister and a missionary.

Perhaps at this point a word concerning the call to any church-related vocation may be appropriately given. There

87

seems to be a tendency with some people to believe that only those who "fight the call" until they can resist it no longer are truly called to such service. Some even affirm that no man should enter the ministry so long as he can stay out of it. They undergird their position by citing Paul's experience. In reply to this idea, it should be remembered that the most commendable part of Paul's experience was not his rebellion against the will of God but his surrender to it in spite of all the forces pulling against his surrender.

Ours would be a far better world and the church would have far better servants if all followers of Christ could remember that to obey the call to do the will of God is not responding to an austere and grim summons; rather is it what Paul says it is, the glad venture of giving oneself to a life of boundless promise, "the promise of life which is in Christ Jesus." For Paul, life could only be found in union with Christ and life on its highest level could only be found in obedience to the will of God made known in Christ. This life is bright with spiritual promise.

Christian optimism is never entirely based on the evidence which all men can trace through an improved earthly order; rather does it rest primarily on the faith that in Christ we live and move and have our being and that one day all things will be reconciled unto him (Col. 1:20). Paul had no grounds for optimism in his imprisonment save the assurance that his true environment was not a prison at all but the vital and real fellowship of Christ. He was, therefore, more than a conqueror in Christ. It is this hope which Paul holds before Timothy as the foremost blessing of the Christian gospel.

## 2. Concern for Timothy

Paul's fellowship with Christ did not preclude his fellowship with men. It would be nearer the truth to say that it necessarily included the fellowship of all men who were in the fellowship of Christ. Paul, therefore, expresses his concern for Timothy, his "dearly beloved son." Paul had been the instrument of God through whom Timothy was born into the family of the redeemed.

The benediction follows: "Grace, mercy, and peace" (1:2). Timothy, by means of his reconciliation with God, had received grace, through which God took the initiative, thus making him gracious. He had received mercy, by which he had been forgiven and made forgiving. This reconciling grace and mercy brought with them God's peace. It is Paul's prayer that Timothy may receive more and more of these heavenly treasures which come "from God the Father and Christ Jesus our Lord" (1:2). It is small wonder that this verse has come to be one of the great benedictions used in our Christian worship today.

## II. GRATITUDE FOR TIMOTHY'S SERVICE (1:3-7)

Timothy's stalwart devotion to Christ was a source of constant inspiration to Paul, so much so that he was grateful even for the memory of him and for the privilege of praying for him.

Paul had served God from his forefathers with "a pure conscience" (1:3 ASV). It now gladdened his heart to find another following in his train. How often Christian prayer is encouraged and made stronger by the memory of others who are laboring with us in the faith. Paul's gratitude arose over the thought of the unbroken lineage of faith which each new generation must make real for itself. The thought of Timothy's fidelity brought boundless assurance to the aged apostle.

What comfort there is in the compassion of others. The tears of Timothy which Paul remembered may have been those which he shed at the farewell at Miletus when Paul took his departure for Rome, as described in Acts 20:37. Few bonds could ever be so strong as those which bound the missionaries of the cross together. The severing of those bonds brought tearful spiritual anguish.

Paul, on the other hand, may have been referring to Timothy's tearful concern over the apostle's imprisonment, or the reference may simply be a description of the anguish through which the heralds of Christ had to pass in order to proclaim the good tidings of God's grace. It is one of the strange paradoxes of the Christian gospel that tears and joy are often joined together.

Perhaps, however, the meaning here (2 Tim. 1:4) is that it is Timothy's tearful devotion to Christ and to the gospel of Christ, for which Paul had given his life, that brought enduring joy to the heart of Paul. In any event, it is the promise of God that "he that goeth forth and weepeth, bearing precious seed, shall doubtless come again with rejoicing, bringing his sheaves with him" (Psalm 126:6).

## 1. Timothy's Religious Heritage

Paul was further grateful for the unfeigned (unhypocritical) faith that Timothy now possessed. It was the sincere faith manifested in his full acceptance of and commitment to the gospel as proclaimed by Paul. Paul's gratitude was deepened by the realization that Christianity now spanned three generations in the family of Timothy and had been guarded and preserved in its pristine purity.

The apostle pays high tribute to Timothy's grandmother Lois, who had passed her faith on to her daughter Eunice, who in turn had passed it on to Timothy. While faith is always a personal matter, family ties are designed of God to make possible the transmission of personal faith within the family in a manner which makes faith grow stronger with each generation.

The strength of the faith of Eunice and Lois was challenged by the fact that Timothy's father was apparently a pagan Greek. If so, then, because of the unbelieving father, the mother and grandmother knew that they had heavier responsibility toward Timothy than would have been true had the father also been a Christian. So careful were they in their training of Timothy that it could later be said to him, "From a child thou hast known the holy scriptures" (2 Tim. 3:15).

When Timothy is later advised to give diligence to "rightly dividing the word of truth" (2 Tim. 2:15), he is called to remember how he was trained in the holy Scriptures.

Dr. Alexander Whyte sees Lois beginning her preparation an hour before she summons in Timothy from the playground. She selects with great care the proper passage she is going to read with him.

> She reads and re-reads the passage to herself, in order to make sure that she understands it herself. After which she prepares, and tries them over on her own knees, two or three petitions proper for the child to repeat after her, and to which he is to say his intelligent and hearty, Amen.[1]

Timothy had known a great religious heritage. He had also been under the personal ministry of Paul and had, no doubt, been ordained to the gospel ministry by Paul and the presbyters at Lystra. Yet faith is not something which can be sustained apart from personal participation and earnest devotion. Faith is not a gift which God gives apart from man's response. It is rather given through enabling man to respond to the overture of divine grace. A human family may be used of God as the means of making the soul sensitive to the divine call, and a good pastor may make the claims of Christ and his offer of salvation most clear, but God can make his gift only as man personally responds in a sustained surrender to Christ.

## 2. *Use of Spiritual Gifts*

Furthermore, the spiritual gifts with which Timothy had been endowed had to be cultivated and put into use before they could be made real. Timothy, therefore, was called upon to "stir up the gift of God" or "rekindle" or "fan into flame" the divine fire which God had kindled in his soul (1:6). When one is called to Christian service he is not immediately made into a marvelous preacher, pastor, or other leader. Neither is he miraculously given abilities which remain static. Rather is he given capacities to be cultivated. Timothy was not called upon, therefore, to create the fire, but to fan it into a living, glowing flame through the constant service into which God had called him.

> We cannot kindle when we will
> The fire which in the heart resides,
> The Spirit bloweth and is still
> In mystery the soul abides.
>
> MATTHEW ARNOLD

Yet we can, through prayer and private devotions, through public worship and positive service, bring into the open spiritual gifts which we never hitherto imagined were in our possession. Only thus can the flame of divine fire be kept bright. The Christian leader who does not study does not know the deepest secrets of prayer. Often the richest experiences of prayer come while concentrating on the holy Scriptures. The voice of God speaks through the written Word and our hearts are lifted up to thank him for his wondrous goodness, and before him we make our vows to follow his divine directive for that day.

True faith imparts a sturdy confidence in God which conquers the fears that often arise in the Christian's heart. Many formidable adversaries arise to strike terror in the heart, and it has been so since the days of Timothy. This young servant of Christ had adequate cause for great fear. He had seen Paul, his father in the ministry, battered and broken and bleeding as he was stoned by the Judaizers outside the gates of Lystra. Moreover, his Lord had been crucified on a rugged Roman cross by Roman soldiers, who were still marching with steady tread to put down any undue excitement and who would brook no hostility in the first-century world.

Still today every Christian has his haunting fears: fear of the opinion of the majority, which is always against the high standards of God; fear of the feeling of insecurity, which always surrounds the soul who has here no abiding city; fear of poverty and of devastating disease, which lay waste the body and derange the mind. The only antidote for the fear which constantly stalks the sensitive Christian soul is shining, steadfast confidence in God. To Christ's servants God gives confidence. God has not given us a spirit of fear nor of timidity. Fear and timidity are the results of seeing our obstacles and our adversaries more clearly than we see God.

### 3. *God-given Courage*

Paul sees God giving to his servants a courage which man could never cultivate for himself. When God bestows his Spirit upon us, fear is superseded and then comes "power," "love," and "self-control [discipline]" (ASV), or sober good sense. Some Christians have placed far too much emphasis exclusively upon the ecstatic gifts of the Spirit of God. This sentence (v. 7) emphasizes the chief gifts of the Spirit: power to do the work to which God has called us; love which enables us to love others as Christ loved them; and self-control, which is that sober good sense which brings the lower side of man's nature under the control of the highest and creates a balance between extremes.

Often when men have power and confidence they blunder brashly and do great damage. On the other hand, when men are controlled by timidity they never undertake the great tasks which God sets before them. If, however, the servants of God have power that is a sustained intensity of life, and love that is the warm outgoing affection and good will for all men, and self-control that is the sober good sense to discipline and balance one's service, then the kingdom of Christ can be steadily and solidly built through such servants. This conquering confidence was often manifested by the early apostles. "Now when they saw the boldness of Peter and John, . . . they took knowledge of them, that they had been with Jesus" (Acts 4:13).

## III. SUFFERING FOR THE GOSPEL (1:8–14)

The Christian gospel has never afforded its adherents a comfortable adjustment with an evil environment. The gospel always creates a tension between men in Christ and men who belong to a world order which crucified Christ. There is little comfort for the Christian who bears witness to a gospel which always causes the majority in the world to scoff.

### 1. A Special Blessing

Timothy must resist the temptation to be ashamed of bearing testimony for his Lord. Even though the chief living advocate of the gospel of the Redeemer was at that time languishing in a Roman prison, still Timothy must not be ashamed. "Rather," says Paul, "must you heroically take your share of the afflictions of the gospel according to the power of God" (1:8).

Our Lord promised a special blessing to those who suffer for him. One of the Beatitudes reads; "Blessed are ye, when men shall revile you, and persecute you, and shall say all manner of evil against you falsely, for my sake. Rejoice, and be exceeding glad: for great is your reward in heaven: for so persecuted they the prophets which were before you" (Matt. 5:11–12).

Timothy was to remember that, although Paul was in prison, still he was kept by the power of God and was being enabled to do more for the glory of Christ in a prison than

others were permitted to do in their unrestrained, open freedom. Timothy then must not allow his fear of imprisonment
to restrain him from boldy preaching the gospel and entering personally into the afflictions of Christ as a result of his
preaching.

## 2. *The Holy Calling*

If Timothy was to maintain his boldness, he must see his
ministry as having its source in the grace of God and its fulfilment in the purpose of God. Timothy had already been
saved in the sense that God in Christ had already moved
into the control of his life and he had been called with a
holy calling which could never be altered. This salvation
was not the result of good works (1:9). In the sense that
God had decisively intervened to remake the life of Timothy,
this young pastor had already been saved. Yet the apostle
was not thinking of salvation solely in terms of its initiation.
He was thinking primarily of the fulfilment of God's total
purpose to which Christian converts are called.

Christians are called to fulfil the "holy calling" by being
holy as God himself is holy. This purpose was in the heart
of God ages ago or "before times eternal." It is grounded in
the very nature of God and does not belong to the temporal
order but is beyond the reach and ruin of time. God's purpose will not be finally thwarted. Therefore, the boldness of
Timothy and of every Christian in proclaiming such a gospel
is securely undergirded.

## 3. *Light on Life and Immortality*

The open manifestation of God's eternal purpose was made
in "the appearing of our Saviour Jesus Christ" (1:10). No
more comprehensive description of the work of the Saviour
appears in the Scriptures than this tenth verse gives, ". . .
our Saviour Jesus Christ, who hath abolished death, and hath
brought life and immortality to light through the gospel."

"The purpose of Christ's coming," says Paul, "was to conquer man's last enemy, death, the king of terrors, and to illumine the whole meaning and reach of life by emphasizing its transcendency over time." Christ entered into the arena of death and vanquished the dark tyrant and united all who trust in him in his triumph over death.

It should be clearly stated that the coming of Jesus of Nazareth did not give to man his belief in immortality. Man had that belief centuries before Jesus was born in Bethlehem; but this much our Lord did accomplish: He enabled men to remove the basis of their belief in immorality from the realm of abstract philosophy and speculation and to center it in the resurrection, which was a concrete historic event. Jesus never argued for immortality on the grounds of earthly analogies, such as the blooming of the lilies, the budding of the branches, and the glories of the springtime. Rather did he center all his hopes in the nature of God.

On one occasion (Matt. 22:29-32) there came to Jesus some Sadducees. They were the intelligentsia of the day. They maintained that the written law alone was of divine authority and obligatory on the nation. They did not believe in the oral traditions of their fathers, nor in the doctrine of the angels, nor in the resurrection of the dead (Acts 23:8). Like most men who handle incomprehensible truth with irreverent minds and unholy hands, many of them were confirmed cynics. Hoping to ensnare Jesus, they came to him with a hypothetical question expressly designed to embarrass him. It was a question predicated on an ancient Jewish custom.

In the tribal days of the Jews, there was placed among the statutes of Israel the requirement that if a man's brother died, he was obligated to take his brother's wife into his own tent and care for her (Deut. 25:5). It was not a moral but an economic problem.

"Now," said the Sadducees, "here is a woman who has

been passed from one brother to another until she has had seven husbands." "Therefore in the resurrection whose wife shall she be of the seven?" (Matt. 22:28). Remember that they did not believe that she would be anybody's wife; they did not believe in the resurrection.

But Jesus said, "Ye do err, not knowing the scriptures, nor the power of God. . . . Have ye not read that which was spoken unto you by God, saying, I am the God of Abraham, and the God of Isaac, and the God of Jacob? God is not the God of the dead, but of the living" (Matt. 22:29–32). These men had been dead for centuries but they were still in the fellowship of God. In other words, that upon which God has set his heart can never die.

The power of God is such and the fellowship of God is so high that it is infinitely better than even the family relationships on earth. "For," said Jesus, "they neither marry, nor are given in marriage" (Matt. 22:30) in the high country of God.

Whether or not one believes in immortality, then, must depend upon what he believes about God. Do you believe that he creates man and invests the treasures of his everlasting grace in man only to desert him at the close of life's weary pilgrimage? Or do you believe that we are bound to God by indissoluble bonds of omnipotent affection? The Saviour is the giver of the new life which comes through the new birth and which does not have death but rather life eternal as its goal.

### 4. Confidence in Christ

The entire purpose of Paul's life is summed up in three terms: He was a preacher of a gospel of a Saviour who has abolished death and brought immortality to light; he was also an apostle or a personal representative of Christ; and he was a teacher of those who were born outside the Jewish tradition, the Gentiles (1:11). For such a gospel Paul was willing to suffer. Indeed, he knew that his calling included the call to suffer.

A gospel of suffering love requires suffering on the part of those who proclaim it. Paul has previously called Timothy not to be ashamed. Now he affirms that he does not consider even his own persecution and imprisonment as shameful. He had staked all on the trustworthiness of God. "For," says he, "I know whom I have believed, and am persuaded that he is able to keep that which I have committed unto him against that day" (1:12). Paul does not contend merely that he knows *what* he believes, but that he knows *whom* he has believed, and that is far better.

John Oxenham expresses this distinction most clearly:

> Not what, but WHOM I do believe,
>   That in my darkest hour of need
>   Hath comfort that no mortal Creed
> To mortal men may give —
> Not what, but WHOM.[2]

JOHN OXENHAM

Paul expresses his confidence in Christ most firmly. The perfect tense translated "have believed" indicates action which is completed in the past but which persists in the present. This is belief which has been tested by experience. Above all else, Paul was certain of the trustworthiness of God. Being fully assured of this, he did not hesitate to entrust his most priceless treasure, his very soul, to God forever. "I am sure," says Paul, "that he is able to keep [to guard] that which I have committed unto him against that day." Here we have the picture of a treasure deposited with one in whom absolute confidence is placed. God's ability to guard this deposit is the final ground of Christian assurance.

Although it is more important to a Christian to know whom he believes, to know what he believes is also highly important. Paul, therefore, appeals to Timothy to "hold fast the form of sound words" (1:13). The word Paul uses for "form" or "pattern" was used to describe the rough draft used by artists. Paul had given Timothy "sound words" which must form the framework of his beliefs and of his own preaching. Even so, Timothy's preaching must not have a hollow secondhand sound. It must be made personal and vital by his own faith and his own love which he personally shared in his union with Christ. Yet for all his personal involvement with the gospel, he must never permit his private opinions to color or distort eternal truth.

Timothy's supreme task was to preserve and transmit unchanged the truth which Paul had deposited in his soul and which the Holy Spirit would keep pure and alive (1:14). In the fourteenth verse we have a clear definition of the manner in which the truth of God has been preserved from one generation to another and of how ancient truth is made real and vital in the present. Truth comes from God in Christ, who revealed himself to the apostles, who in turn guarded his message and passed it on to faithful witnesses in whom the Holy Spirit moved, to preserve and to interpret for the personal needs of every believer in every generation.

## IV. Paul's Personal Friendships (1:15–18)

Paul knew how much the spread of the gospel was dependent upon personal friendships which unite men into a indissoluble loyalty. To strengthen the bonds of his friendship with Timothy and to encourage Timothy's loyalty, Paul portrays the blackness of his abandonment. Paul felt that all who were in Asia had deserted him. He, therefore, clung most desperately to the few friends whom he had left.

### 1. The Desertion of Some Former Friends

What happened to Paul has happened to many a Christian leader. The passage in Acts 19 and 20 tells us of Paul's great success in Asia as he centered his ministry in Ephesus. Now, in his hour of need, he says, "All they which are in

Asia be turned away from me." It seems that Christian workers are expendable but the gospel marches on.

It seems hardly possible that this passage could mean that all of Paul's converts in Asia had forsaken his doctrine or had ceased to be friendly toward him. More likely, the reference is simply to those who were most close to Paul, whom the aged apostle had expected would communicate with him. The meaning could be "those from Asia" and would, therefore, be a reference to Christians from Asia but dwelling in Rome, who cared for Paul for a while, then, fearing that they might be imprisoned, abondoned him to his fate.

We have no way of knowing who Phygellus and Hermogenes were, since they are named only here (1:15). They probably were persons whom Timothy knew and who, Paul regrets to report, forsook him when he needed them most. They were Paul's "fair-weather" friends.

## 2. *The Kindness of Onesiphorus*

When one is deserted and desolate, acts of kindness are deeply appreciated. There was one friend whose kindness to Paul has been handed down to us to encourage similar courtesies to the servants of Christ who are in need. Onesiphorus, according to tradition, had been won to Christ by Paul during his ministry at Iconium. Onesiphorus did not forget his indebtedness to Paul. Unlike those who were ashamed of his chains and deserted him, Onesiphorus and his family refreshed the apostle. As Moffat translates it, "Many a time he braced me up" (1:16).

Paul's wish, "the Lord give mercy unto the house of Onesiphorus," is simply the desire for the fulfilment of the word of Christ, "Blessed are the merciful: for they shall obtain mercy" (Matt. 5:7). Paul's reference to his chains suggests that his refreshment came through the personal visit of his friend or of the members of the family of Onesiphorus to his prison.

The diligent search for Paul by Onesiphorus (1:17) indicates that Paul's second imprisonment in Rome was in the "inner prison," to which the public was not invited. Not even the members of the church knew of the exact place of his imprisonment. Only after the most thorough search did Onesiphorus find him. For all his sacrificial search and for his tender ministries, Paul prays that Onesiphorus may find mercy from the Lord in the day of judgment. The chapter closes with a grateful tribute to Onesiphorus for his manifold ministries to Paul at Ephesus.

## SUGGESTIONS FOR STUDY AND DISCUSSION

1. Discuss the proper attitude toward the will of God.
2. Discuss the factors at work in the conversion of Timothy.
3. Show how the promises of modern religious prophets regarding a comfortable adjustment with an evil environment contradict the teachings of Paul.
4. Discuss how the resurrection of Jesus brought "immortality to light" (2 Tim. 1:10).

[1] Alexander Whyte, *Bible Characters* (London: Oliphants, Ltd., 1952), II, p. 300. Used by permission.

[2] John Oxenham, "Credo," *Bees in Amber* (New York: American Tract Society, 1917). Used by permission of Miss Erica Oxenham, copyright owner.

## CHAPTER 8

I. THE NEED FOR DILIGENCE (2:1–7)

    1. Obligation Based on Heritage
    2. A Suffering Soldier
    3. A Disciplined Athlete
    4. An Industrious Farmer

II. THE DEATH THAT BRINGS LIFE (2:8–13)

    1. Harmony Between the Teachings of Paul and Jesus
    2. The Centrality of Christ's Death and Resurrection
    3. The Eternal Glory

III. THE WORD OF TRUTH (2:14–19)

    1. The Workman Unashamed
    2. A Spurious Concept of Progress
    3. Paul's View of the Spiritual Body

# 8

# *The Death That Brings Life*

## I. THE NEED FOR DILIGENCE (2:1–7)

Timothy's obligation to be a good soldier of Jesus Christ stemmed out of his heritage as a child of faith (2 Tim. 1:5); his holy calling from God and his ordination by the church (1:6); and his endowment of power, love, and a sound mind (1:7). He had been "braced up" by the example of Paul's faithfulness to the gospel and by the devotion of Onesiphorus to Paul. Paul gathers up all this heritage in his call, "Thou therefore, my son, be strong in the grace that is in Christ Jesus" (2:1). As others had found strength in the grace that is in Christ which enabled them to endure, so Timothy could find his responsibilities matched with adequate strength.

### 1. *Obligation Based on Heritage*

Timothy was indebted to Paul and to the many witnesses who had brought him to Christ and confirmed his convictions. Even so, he must transmit the Christian message to other faithful men who would accept the call to service and would guard the sacred truth with their very lives and compassionately pass it on to others. Constantly he must give himself to developing the members of his church so that they might give themselves "unto the work of ministering, unto the building up of the body of Christ" (Eph. 4:12 ASV).

One of the foremost tasks of the Christian minister is to

encourage those who have been called of God to enter vigorously into their calling. The experienced minister must give much time and attention to the younger generation of ministers that they may be able worthily to teach others. Some ministers have enormous ability to "call out the called."

While no one would wish any man to be in the ministry —or in any church-related vocation—unless he has been called of God, it is the solemn responsibility of men of God to help others to recognize the call of the Lord and to surround them with the help that will enable them to fulfil their high calling. Men of God should, therefore, be alert to discern spiritually sensitive young people whom God may be calling and to encourage these young people to answer God's call. Thus, the spiritual succession of the servants of Christ may be carried on, as competent and trustworthy teachers of the truth of Christ learn the truth and commit themselves to pass it on.

The importance of finding such Christian workers who will pass on the truth is emphasized in three analogies. In verses 3–6 Paul likens these Christian leaders to the soldier, the athlete, and the farmer. Diligence is a vital factor in the success in any of these professions, and so it is in the Christian ministry.

## 2. A Suffering Soldier

First of all, the apostle reminds Timothy that the ordinary experience of a soldier is to suffer. If one is to be a good soldier of Christ, he must take his share of suffering. A good soldier is regarded as an outstanding example of self-sacrifice, steadfast loyalty, and absolute devotion to his country. Even so, a good soldier of Jesus Christ must embody this sacrificial loyalty and devotion to the kingdom of heaven.

Every good pastor is in constant conflict against the adversary. He, therefore, has no time for civilian pursuits. He cannot leave the battle to invest in real estate, nor to entertain the local clubs, nor to give his time to lesser pursuits when the powers of darkness are assaulting the citadels of men's souls. As long as the battle rages he must be at the hot fighting front in order that Christ, "who enlisted him," might be pleased.

This is a clear example of the truth that "men of God" should be wholly engaged in the work to which they are called and not scatter their efforts so thinly among secular pursuits that their ministry is dissipated. It is, of course, commendable that men who are called of God should labor with their hands in the making of a living that they might preach the gospel in areas where churches are not strong enough to support them. On the other hand, every church should be taught that this means of pastorial support is not the highest will of God. The church which realizes this fact and deliberately refuses to support a pastor, sins most grievously against God and against the souls of men to whom the pastor should minister.

### 3. *A Disciplined Athlete*

In the fifth verse, Paul emphasizes the truth that although an athlete may strive ever so successfully, yet he is not awarded the winner's crown unless he competes according to the rules. The athlete must discipline himself to obey rugged training rules and in the contest must carefully obey the regulations. If this is true of an athlete how much more important is it that one who seeks a heavenly crown and who has been carefully instructed in the rules for his ministry shall observe them.

Regarding the rigors of discipline needed, Paul wrote, on another occasion: "Any man who enters an athletic contest practices rigid self-control in training, only to win a wreath that withers. . . . That is the way I run, with no uncertainty as to winning. That is the way I box, not like one who punches the air. But I keep on beating and bruising my body and making it my slave, so that I, after I have summoned others to the race, may not myself become unfit to run" (1 Cor. 9:25-27 Williams).[1]

### 4. An Industrious Farmer

In the sixth verse, Paul insists that it is the farmer who has done the hard work who ought to have the first share of the crops. Only the hard working farmer can expect good crops. Even so a good minister of Christ must toil diligently. Many times in the New Testament the agricultural metaphor is used to prove the right of a pastor to receive financial support from his people (1 Tim. 5:17-18; 1 Cor. 9:3-14). This passage, therefore, has a twofold emphasis: The pastor must work hard and the congregation must supply his needs.

The three proverbs may be summarized as follows: As a good soldier the pastor must suffer hardships, as an athlete he must minister according to the rules, and as a farmer he must work hard from early until late if he is to gain the harvest. These proverbs have many more implications. Paul, therefore, calls Timothy to consider them well that the deeper meanings may be made known to him as the Lord grants him understanding. Unquestionably, the application of the principles set forth is not limited to pastors.

## II. THE DEATH THAT BRINGS LIFE (2:8-13)

The apostle's appeal, "remember Jesus Christ" (2:8 ASV), along with the reference to Jesus' descent from David, reveals Paul's interest in the earthly life of the Man of Nazareth. The earthly story, however, is not complete apart from the resurrection of the Redeemer.

### 1. Harmony Between the Teachings of Paul and Jesus

Many have been the attempts to prove that what Paul thought about Jesus Christ and what the Man of Nazareth taught about himself were radically different. An honest examination of the Pauline Scriptures, however, will reveal that the apostle constantly sought to lead his readers back to the historic Jesus and to the greatest of historic events, his death and resurrection. Paul's gospel is not simply a story of a Man who lived sublimely in the long ago and far away. Rather is it the story of one whose life did not begin at Bethlehem nor end on Golgotha. It is the story of the Eternal coming into time, of God becoming man, and of the eternal nearness of the man Christ Jesus to every trusting heart.

## 2. *The Centrality of Christ's Death and Resurrection*

The focal point of the Pauline gospel is the cross and the resurrection. The man Christ Jesus died, therefore, he must have had a beginning. Yet there was something unique about the ending of the earthly life of Jesus. It did not really end. It was lifted up in a glorified body and was manifested among the followers of Christ so convincingly that amazing moral and spiritual transformations took place in the lives of men who had walked with him in the flesh, but who were now walking in the power of his risen fellowship. Never had mankind known such experience before. Therefore, Paul could see that the life that Jesus had did not belong to the sphere of time but to eternity. It came from above the temporal and it reaches backward into God's eternity and forward into God's eternity when time shall be no more. His life was ultimately above the reach and ruin of the temporal order.

## 3. *The Eternal Glory*

For such a gospel Paul was willing to suffer personally the degradation of imprisonment, for he was fully assured that the gospel can never be bound. Men may suffer and even perish from the earth for the sake of the message, but no earthly fetters can ever restrain nor limit the freedom of the gospel. Even if the earthly voices which proclaim it go down in silence, the Word of God has supernatural power to make its impact upon the conscience of man through the Holy Spirit; thus the church continues to have her gospel despite the failures of her pastors (2:9).

Paul knew that the very doctrine of grace means that God has taken the initiative and has determined that salvation is totally to be the work of God, insomuch that even man's response, while truly his, is due to the enabling grace of God; and Paul knew that God's purpose to save would finally be fulfilled. Because of this knowledge, he was enabled steadfastly to endure all things. His suffering was linked with God's eternal purpose, which cannot fail. Paul was content to take the toil and the hardship, for he was perfectly assured that beyond it, for himself and for all the chosen sons of God, would be eternal glory (2:10). This eternal glory is a life of unhindered, triumphant fellowship with God, which is beyond the reach of death.

In so many cases did the early converts to Christianity find it necessary to draw comfort from the most basic truth of the gospel that an oft-quoted part of the liturgy of the early church came to be: "It is a faithful saying: For if we be dead with him, we shall also live with him" (2:11). To die with Christ is to do what the ancient psalmist described as walking "through the valley of the shadow" (Psalm 23:4). Death for those in Christ is not a blind alley but an open thoroughfare to God's upper kingdom.

This eleventh verse, however, is probably meant primarily to describe the symbolic death of those who enter into union with Christ through repentance. Paul thought of repentance as death to the old life of sin. The Christian is called to die *to* sin as completely as Christ died *for* sin. To be crucified with Christ means utterly to renounce and to refuse to make terms with sin, which crucified the Redeemer. To be dead to sin is to be beyond the domination of that which destroys the soul. It is to have entered the conquering fellowship of

Christ. Death to sin is, in a sense, the measure of our union with Christ, for only Christ can enable us to die to sin.

There is a rhythm in Williams' translation of 2 Timothy 2:11–13 [editor's arrangement]:

> This message is to be trusted:
> "If we indeed have died with Him,
>    we will live with Him too.
> If we patiently endure,
>    we will reign with Him too.
> If we disown Him,
>    He will disown us too.
> If we are unfaithful, He remains faithful,
>    for He cannot prove false to Himself." [2]

Verses 11–13 probably compose an early Christian hymn which was meant to assure the worshipers of the faithfulness of God and which was sung at baptismal services. Verse 11 is virtually a repetition of Romans 6:8, the explanation of which may be found in Romans 6:3–5. Baptism portrays the death of the Christian with Christ and the sharing of the resurrection of his Lord. The new life of a Christian is so radically different that Paul could only describe it in terms of resurrection. In Colossians 3:1, he writes: "If ye then be risen with Christ, seek those things which are above." Eternal life for Paul was that new quality of life which begins now in the fellowship of the risen Lord and reaches on into God's everlasting tomorrow.

This death to sin must be continual. The baptismal confession marks only the beginning of an enduring experience of repentance and faith. The word "suffer" in verse 12 is better translated "endure." "If we endure with him we shall also reign with him." The New Testament always teaches that genuine faith will be persevering faith. "He that endureth to the end shall be saved" (Matt. 10:22). Only the steadfast perseverance of a Christian can demonstrate that he has saving faith, and only faith that endures is saving faith. Only those who endure will share in the final reign of Christ in his kingdom of glory.

In contrast with this splendid promise, there stands the austere warning against faithlessness: "If we deny him, he also will deny us" (2:12). This statement clearly recalls the Master's words: "But whosoever shall deny me before men, him will I also deny before my Father which is in heaven" (Matt. 10:33). This denial is made all the more dreadful in that it is promised to those who have had the opportunity to become sharers of Christ's everlasting glory, yet who have denied Christ.

The austerity of this warning is accentuated in the thirteenth verse: "If we believe not, yet he abideth faithful; he cannot deny himself." Paul seems to emphasize the well-nigh universal refusal of man to believe that Christ could ever deny them a share in his glory. This verse emphatically stresses the normal self-consistency of God. Whether or not we believe it, God knows this to be true and he cannot deny what he has spoken; "if we deny him, he also will deny us."

## III. The Word of Truth (2:14–19)

Again Paul solemnly warns Timothy of the futility of disputing about words. The Holy Spirit rarely speaks in a climate of controversy. "Word fighting" with heretical teachers is a sham battle. Only the spirit of compassionate concern for those who are in the bondage of false religious doctrine will create the climate through which the Spirit of truth may speak.

The approved workman will not deplete his energies by entering into futile conflicts either with "heresy hunters" or heretics. He will rather, give himself to a personal mastery of the truth through diligent study. His concern should not be to demonstrate his superb dialectical skill but rather to have the smile of God's approval as a competent workman" (2:15).

### 1. *The Workman Unashamed*

The word translated "dividing" or "handling" (2:15 ASV) originally meant "to cut straight," as a farmer who drives his furrow straight or a tailor who scrupulously cuts the cloth according to the pattern. Timothy, therefore, was to take the gospel and cut straight through its meaning without irrelevant wandering, and present the straight truth of God. The proper handling of the Word of Truth, according to Paul, is to study it, personally appropriate it, and preach the straight truth of it.

In so doing, Timothy would avoid the "profane and vain babblings [godless chatter]" (2:16), which lead people into more and more ungodliness. Dr. Moffatt describes this as "profane jargon." The reference is probably to an attempt within the church to accommodate distinctive Christian truths to the current philosophical concepts.

"This attempt," says Paul, "can only lead to the perverting of the true doctrine by subordinating the revealed truth of God to a speculative system which prided itself as being the product of superior minds and, therefore, it was claimed, could only be appreciated by superior minds."

### 2. *A Spurious Concept of Progress*

Sophisticated people puffed up in their empty pride have often persuaded themselves that the sole concern of true religion is to exercise the intellect in the understanding of highly complicated metaphysical formulas. They are the people who delight to talk about the "deep things" and "deep sermons." Their folly is that in their speculative approach to revealed truth they cut the very historical foundations out from under our faith and leave us in such bottomless depths that we can never be certain about anything.

The result of such an approach to religion is always increased ungodliness (2:16). It is the same strategy used by the builders of the tower of Babel. The only difference is the reversal in direction. If man's attempt to climb up to heaven by his own unaided intellect is sheer folly, then man's attempt to dig into the deep things of God with the same unaided intellect is equal folly.

The word translated "increase" or "lead" (2:16) depicts the flippant concept of religious progress which has plagued the soul of man since the days of Adam. The multitude of religious cults are the products of man's departure from the truth "once for all delivered unto the saints" (Jude 3 ASV) and of man's pride which leads him to seek to improve on eternal truth.

Man's impatience with revealed truth stems out of the heavy demands it makes upon him. He seeks to comfort himself by rationalizing away these demands and by creating a new creed for himself. This, he persuades himself to believe, is progress, but it is only progress toward more and more ungodliness. This approach to religion works like a fatal disease and will ultimately destroy the church, since it does not feed, rather does it feed upon, the church.

Paul calls the names of two of these heretical teachers, Hymenaeus and Philetus. These two teachers had erred in their interpretation of the most vital Christian doctrine, the resurrection. They contended "that the resurrection is past already" (2:18). This controversy in the early church did not gather around the fact of the resurrection, but around the time of the resurrection. It seems that Hymenaeus and Philetus embraced a part of Paul's teaching but not all. They embraced that part which would be in keeping with the teachings of the Greeks who believed in immortality and in judgment after death.

### 3. *Paul's View of the Spiritual Body*

Salvation, for the Greek, was the release of the indestructible soul from its prison house to a glorious freedom and true fulfilment. The Greeks thought of flesh as something which circumscribed and maddened the spirit. The beauty of the soul could not be revealed until it was unhampered by the body. To think of the soul being again imprisoned in a body by the resurrection was unspeakably vulgar to the Greeks. This is the reason the Athenians mocked Paul when he spoke on the resurrection (Acts 17:32).

On the other hand, the Hebrew teaching was that the body was created by a good and righteous God. It could not, therefore, of itself be evil. Since the Hebrew thought of the total personality of man as body and soul, and since he believed in the total redemption of man, he believed that the body would share in immortality at the resurrection.

Now Paul believed in a spiritual body (1 Cor. 15:44). He believed that Christ came to redeem the total life of man, body and soul. He, however, did hold to a lower view of the natural body than did rabbinical Judaism. Frequently he referred to the natural body in a symbolic sense, as: "Flesh and blood cannot inherit the kingdom of God" (1 Cor. 15:50). "They that are in the flesh cannot please God" (Rom. 8:8). This natural body must, therefore, come under the control of the Spirit. Paul believed that if the Spirit of God dwells in a man, that man is no longer "in the flesh, but in the Spirit" (Rom. 8:9–14).

Paul believed in a spiritual regeneration through faith in Christ, which brings the believer into a risen life of fellowship with the risen Christ, in which man is no longer dominated by the flesh (Col. 3:1). Paul also believed in a resurrection of the dead at the coming of Christ (1 Cor. 15:15–54). At this time will come full and final redemption as the dead are raised. "The dead shall be raised incorruptible, and we shall be changed" (1 Cor. 15:52). The body of the resurrection will not be the weak, dishonorable, physical body, but a glorified body—a redeemed body capable of fulfilling the purposes of a redeemed spirit.

Now the heresy of Hymenaeus and Philetus lay, probably, in the fact that they accepted only the first half of Paul's doctrine, his belief in spiritual resurrection, which they equated with the Greek doctrine of immortality, while they denied the future resurrection of the body and the total redemption of man at the final coming of Christ. They would thus have been akin to those among us who say, "One world at a time. I have no interest in life after death nor in the long reaches of an incalculable eternity." They were thus touching one of the dearest hopes of the Christian church, that of the blessed reunion with Christ and his saints.

Despite all who would destroy the church by disputation (2:16) and by false teaching (2:18), and even despite the fact that some within the church have had their faith overthrown, the foundation of God, the true religion which the church has received, stands secure. It cannot be ruined nor finally upset. The true religion of Christ is the cornerstone of the church and the "seal" or the inscription which describes the nature of the church. The church is Christ's own body. He surely "knoweth them that are his" (2:19). Because God knows all men perfectly, such knowledge Paul sees as a solemn warning to all teachers to depart from the sin of "swerving from the truth."

Men may deceive themselves into thinking that they know God and understand the truth of God. "Yet" says Paul, "God can never be deceived in his knowledge of the human heart and of the sincerity of a person's devotion to him." Verse 19 is thus a recollection of the words of Jesus, "Not every one that saith unto me, Lord, Lord, shall enter into the kingdom of heaven; but he that doeth the will of my Father which is in heaven. Many will say to me in that day, Lord, Lord, have we not . . . in thy name done many wonderful works? And then will I profess unto them, I never knew you: depart from me, ye that work iniquity" (Matt. 7:21–23).

## SUGGESTIONS FOR STUDY AND DISCUSSION

1. Show how a good pastor is like a soldier, an athlete, and a farmer. Discuss the application of these analogies to other Christian leaders.
2. Discuss the background of Paul's statement, "It is a faithful saying" (2 Tim. 2:11).
3. Let the class take hymn books and find Christian hymns which carry the message of 2 Timothy 2:11.
4. Discuss the pictorial significance of Christian baptism.

---

[1] Charles B. Williams, *The New Testament in the Language of the People* (Chicago: Moody Press, 1955). Used by permission.
[2] *Ibid.*

# CHAPTER 9

I. MEET FOR THE MASTER'S USE (2:20–26)

    1. Use of Imperfect Utensils
    2. Prerequisites for the Highest Service
    3. Responsibilities of Christian Youth
    4. The Minister's Teaching Ministry

II. CONDUCT IN THE LAST DAYS (3:1–9)

    1. The Unending Struggle
    2. Description of False Teachers

III. PAUL'S EXAMPLE (3:10–13)

    1. Accurate Teaching and Vivid Example
    2. God's Invincible Purpose
    3. Delivery Through Persecution

IV. THE SCRIPTURAL FOUNDATIONS OF TRUE FAITH (3:14–17)

    1. Steadfast Adherence to Factual Side of Faith
    2. The Immutable Standard

V. THE CHRISTIAN WORKER'S SOLEMN CHARGE (4:1–5)

    1. A Pastor Awaiting Judgment
    2. Rebuking Error
    3. No Popularity Promised

# 9

# The Pastor's Solemn Charge

## I. MEET FOR THE MASTER'S USE (2:20–26)

One of the baffling questions continually confronting the Christian church is this: Why does God permit such dissenters and disturbers of the Christian fellowship as Hymenaeus and Philetus to teach in the church?

### 1. *Use of Imperfect Utensils*

Of course, it could never be concluded that God desires false teachers to lead his people. On the other hand, we must patiently remember that should our Lord accept only perfect teachers in his church there would be none to carry on his work. Furthermore, just as the church is not a fellowship of perfect people, even so the ministry is composed of men of like passions with all their human kindred. Perhaps God permits such men to teach because there is always the possibility of their repenting and accepting the truth.

Paul emphasizes this truth in metaphorical language. As in a large mansion there would be various utensils serving various purposes and consequently being of varying values, even so the churches have ministers of many kinds and of differing worth. Some are like vessels made of wood and earth. Others are like vessels made of gold and silver. Some are true to their commission and are "honorable." Others distort the doctrine delivered unto them and are, therefore, "dishonorable." Yet even the most dishonorable, by purifying himself through the means which God has provided, through genuine repentance, may become like a vessel of gold and silver, a vessel of honor.

Some commentators see the inconsistency of such a metaphor, contending that the composition of a vessel cannot be changed from earthenware to gold simply by cleansing. It must be remembered, however, that divine cleansing is a miracle of radical transformation. To change the human heart is as dramatic a miracle as it would be to change earthenware into gold. To make a good and true servant of Jesus Christ is like taking a common vessel used in the most menial of tasks and transforming it into a magnificent gold or silver vessel like unto those used in the ceremonies of sacrifices in the temple. When a person is sanctified or set apart and made "meet for the Master's use" there is no God-given task for which he will not be equal. When God sets his servants apart and calls them into his service, he also prepares them for "every good work" (2:21).

"If a man therefore purge himself from these," more immediately means his deliberate severing himself from the "godless chatter" and "profane jargon" of verse 16, by which the Christian faith was being accommodated to the prevailing philosophy of the time and thus fused into a syncretism which, for all its noble elements, still represented man's vain attempt to bring God down totally into the grasp of human reason.

## 2. Prerequisites for the Highest Service

To be "meet for the Master's use" a minister, or other Christian worker, must remember the prerequisites for Christian service laid down by his Master. They are (1) true penitence (Luke 18:14), which must be practiced daily as a man of God dies daily not only to the glory which surrounds the ministry and puffs up with pride, but also to the criticism which will beat his spirit down into the dust; (2) the child-like heart (Matt. 18:3); (3) genuine spiritual discernment (Matt. 6:19–20, 33); (4) total commitment (Luke 14:26); (5) true compassion (Matt. 22:36–39); and (6) sturdy faith (Matt. 17:20).

### 3. Responsibilities of Christian Youth

In 1 Timothy 4:12, Paul reminded Timothy, "Let no man despise thy youth." He was then interested in Timothy's employing his youthful enthusiasm and vigor in positive pursuits which would further the gospel and build Christ's kingdom. Youth has its boundless potentialities but it also has its perils. It is full of passion. This passion is not only in the realm of the flesh but also in the realm of the spirit, sometimes causing youthful leaders to be restive and recalcitrant, impulsive and rebellious, resenting authority, intrigued by novelty, and impatient with tradition—all of which stirs up strife in the church and breaks the most precious of all the church's human possessions, her fellowship.

Youthful passions may be sublimated by the positive pursuit of righteousness, faith, charity, and peace and by remaining loyal to that great fellowship of Christians who have refused to follow Hymenaeus and other such instigators of strife in the Christian congregation.

The whole burden of this appeal lies in Paul's concern that Timothy may respect the nature of the unchangeable truth of God and not be tempted impulsively to distort it and thus break the fellowship of the church. He must remain in that unbroken fellowship with those who call upon the Lord with "pure," meaning orthodox, hearts.

### 4. The Minister's Teaching Ministry

The Lord's servant must steer clear of questions which breed quarrels (2:24). He must be sympathetic with men who are unlearned, and recognize that their questions do not merit the effort that is required for a heated controversy. The more productive approach is that of a gentle, patient, kindly concern for the questioner, which realizes that the mission of the servant of the Lord is to win men not arguments. The offensive bludgeoning of an opponent by a barrage of superior knowledge and of dialectical skill does not draw men to him of whom it was said, "A bruised reed shall he not break, and smoking flax shall he not quench" (Matt. 12:20).

An apt teacher is not one who pours forth the venom of rash hostility upon the ignorant and slow of mind, thus inviting them to put up their defenses and compelling them to fight back. Only the patient and forbearing can be the Lord's servants, or the Lord's "slaves" (2:24). Slaves are under bondage. They, therefore, have no right to indulge themselves in an arrogance which contradicts the spirit of their Master and breaks the fellowship of the church which he died to build.

Only the meek (2:25) are good instructors of the Christian faith, for they realize that they are not the creators of Christian truth, they are only the vessels through which it is carried to others. Neither can they produce repentance which leads to the acknowledging of the truth. Only God can do this, therefore, what place can there be for prideful arrogance which runs roughshod over the opponents to trample them into submission? The way of God is described in the Word of God, "Come now, and let us reason together" (Isa. 1:18).

The word "meek" originally signified a wild horse which had been tamed. The meek in the kingdom of heaven are those who still have the passionate concern and fiery motivation but who have given these into the control of Christ. They are, therefore, the steady, disciplined, dependable channels through which God may send his truth with the assurance that pride will never create a controversy that will clog the channel nor color the truth.

Only through such teachers may men "come to their senses" (2:26 Moffatt). The rebellion of men against the truth that is in Christ is irrational and is the result of moral madness. It was said of the Prodigal that it was "when he came to himself, he said, . . . I will arise and go to my father" (Luke 15:17–18). Paul saw the opponents of the Christian truth as having been caught in the devil's snare to do his will. If a Christian leader is meek, patient, and gentle, through him God can create repentance in his opponent's heart and bring the opponent to his senses and into the glorious liberty of the children of God.

It is no accident that a well developed training program in a church unifies its activities, develops members with strong doctrinal convictions, produces soul-winners, and results in numerical and spiritual growth.

## II. CONDUCT IN THE LAST DAYS (3:1–9)

Having shown the proper manner of dealing with error, the apostle moves on to assure Timothy that the struggle will continue to the very end. Paul did not seek to bolster the spirit of Timothy for battle against corrupt and heretical teachers by depicting the inexorable march of truth which would beat down all error in the Christian community. Rather did he call Timothy to be strong enough to fight to the end in the truceless conflict against false teachers.

### 1. *The Unending Struggle*

Paul shows why this conflict will continue even to "the last days," which in Apocalyptic literature designate the period at the end of this present age, which will come finally to a close with the return of Christ in the fullness of his glory. This conflict is an expression of the universal corruption of this evil world.

It seems to this writer, however, that Paul's chief concern was not so much to deal in detail with the perilous times which will precede the coming of Christ as to explain to Timothy why he must continue to deal with false teachers who opposed the truth. Since, says Paul, the whole moral universe is tinged with evil, Timothy must not be astonished at the prevalence and power of evil teachers.

## 2. *Description of False Teachers*

In times of great stress, normal restraints are flung to the winds and the laws of God and men are flouted and defied. Anarchy is the result. Every man does that which is right in his own eyes, which means that he repudiates all traditional outside guidance and indulges his own whims. "They are lovers of their own selves" (3:2). When man loves self more than God he becomes his own god, and the pathos of this fact is that he is left with such an inadequate god. Out of love of self comes covetousness, for lovers of self must pamper themselves. Centering all their worship in themselves, they become proud, overbearing, abusive scoffers.

To the Jews, next to the sin of disobeying God was the sin of disobeying parents. This was true because the father was the absolute authority in his own home and over his own household. To repudiate his authority represented the most grievous anarchy. The man who acknowledges no power above him has no one to whom to be grateful. He, therefore, loses the grace of gratitude. Ingratitude leads to a repudiation of God and to an unholy denial of all things sacred.

To refuse to acknowledge the sacred side of life is also to lose the human side (3:3), for these men, says Paul, "are inhuman, unsympathetic, without natural affection." Their hearts have turned to stone. They are irreconcilable, "trucebreakers." At this point Paul uses a word which originally meant "without libation or drink offering." It came eventually to mean "without a truce," which was sealed by a libation. Finally, it came to mean "implacable," "refusing to halt hostilities." Such men could not be reconciled to God nor man because their chosen course had brought them to a state of insensibility to spiritual motivations.

"False accusers," or slanderers were those who deliberately lied and thus instigated quarrels. "Incontinent" means profligates, those licentious persons who had lost all self-control. The "fierce" were men who had become hard and brutal (3:3). The "despisers" of good had so degenerated that they were no longer capable of affection for anything.

The pattern of degeneration continually deepens, and Paul speaks of "traitors," those treacherous souls who would betray their best friends (3:4). The "heady," or reckless, are those headstrong souls who will let nothing prevent them from having their own way. The "highminded" are those who are so swollen with conceit that they are literally wrapped up in conceit and folly. They are so introverted that they cannot see objectively outside of themselves at all.

All such men, according to Paul, are fundamentally insincere in their religion. They have "a form of godliness" (religion) but deny "the power thereof." They take the vocabulary of religion but refuse the reality which it expresses. They read their own meaning into the religious symbols and forms because they cannot truly commit themselves to the reality behind the forms.

They claim to be orthodox in their doctrine, yet they deny the very heart and center of the Christian faith, which is the reality of the risen Redeemer, who dwells within the trusting heart to provide power for the remaking of life. "The power" (3:5) which the New Testament proclaims is the power that brought Chirst out of the grave and which enters into every soul committed to Christ (3:5). Without such power the Christian religion is an empty shell.

Verse 5 is often interpreted to refer to men who embrace the factual side of religion. Yet it may be that the men whom Paul had in mind were those described in the preceding chapter (2:18). If so, they were ardent proclaimers of their heresy, since they declared everywhere that the resurrection was past already (2 Tim. 2:18). Paul appeals, therefore, to Timothy to see that such men are simply working in their own power, offering others a powerless religion. He must then turn away from them, avoid them.

Paul did not mean that Timothy was to refuse to associate with the false teachers and to give up the attempt to lead them to the truth. Rather did he mean that Timothy, as one who would be choosing leaders in the infant churches, must not choose men who denied the heart of the Christian gospel that in union with Christ men can find resurrection power in the present moment, in death, and beyond deatth.

From the detailed description of false teachers who publicly proclaim their heresies, Paul moves on to the subtler teachers who creep into houses to "take captive silly women" or literally "little women." Perhaps the apostle is here referring to the vulnerability of some women, who, not being permitted to speak in public, would be flattered by the personal visitation of a prominent leader in their own homes. These false teachers would work insiduously in the homes and would thus gain a following and infiltrate the church with their doctrines. Paul sees women who are so easily led astray as fickle persons who are prone to evil. They are "laden," or heaped up, with sins and are "wayward creatures of impulse" (3:6 Moffatt), utterly devoid of moral stability.

Persons who lack spiritual stability are easy prey for heretical teachers for they do not know their own minds. They are "always learning" in the sense that they have never really learned anything (3:7). In the moral and spiritual realm, knowledge is not merely the conclusions one forms at the close of intellectual research. It is rather the result of exercising the will to cause one's pattern of life to conform to the truth which has been revealed. The indiscriminating people who flit from one fad and fancy to another, willing to listen to anybody, "always learning," never come to the knowledge of the truth because they would rather flit to some new fancy than face the moral demands of the truth already revealed to them.

Paul cites as examples of such fickleness Jannes and Jambres who, although not mentioned in the Old Testament, are identified in early Christian literature as two Egyptian magicians who, by performing countermiracles in the courts of Pharaoh, sought to thwart the efforts of Moses to liberate the Israelites. Paul's point is that these men did not succeed and neither will false teachers, for all their subtlety and insidious craftiness, succeed.

## III. PAUL'S EXAMPLE (3:10–13)

In the midst of a multitude of false teachers, Paul saw one true light burning brightly in the person of Timothy, who had by Paul's careful personal instructions been prepared to preach the truth. He had come to know the truth by following it in his own life.

### 1. *Accurate Teaching and Vivid Example*

The Greek word translated "fully known," or "observed" means literally "to follow," to "act on the basis of." One must practice the ethics of the gospel or he cannot know the theological truth of the gospel. Timothy knew both what Paul taught in theory and how he manifested his teaching in his personal conduct. It is always easier to imitate an example than it is to embrace a theory. Timothy had the dual advantage of accurate teaching and of vivid example. He knew what Paul taught the churches in the name of Christ and also how Paul had administered the affairs of the churches.

### 2. *God's Invincible Purpose*

Furthermore, Timothy had come to share Paul's "purpose" or his intentions and convictions. The four cardinal virtues of Christianity—"faith"; "longsuffering," or patience; "charity," or love; and "patience," or steadfastness (3:10)—had been richly exemplified in Paul and were now developing in Timothy as he manifested the Christian growth which delighted Paul's heart.

## 3. *Delivery Through Persecution*

Timothy had no doubt suffered persecutions with Paul, and could well remember the price the apostle had paid for his devotion to Christ. Paul reminds him that before they had ever met he had also suffered great persecutions at Antioch, Iconium, and Lystra (3:11). Since Timothy's home was at Lystra, he had probably many times heard reports of the persecution of Paul there. Probably these reports played their part in the conversion of Timothy, for he could not have forgotten the fact that it was at Lystra that Paul was stoned and left for dead outside the city gates (Acts 14:8–20).

"Out of them all the Lord delivered me" (v. 11) is a reminder to Timothy that God's purpose in the lives of his followers will not be thwarted by persecutions. Although Paul finally gave his life for his faith, it was not until God's purpose for him was finished. "Earnest devotion to Christ must necessarily," says Paul, "bring persecution." E. F. Scott paraphrases verse twelve, "All who resolve to be Christians in real earnest shall suffer persecutions." [1] These, however, will continue in Christ Jesus and this is their reward.

The Christian message is not that Christian men shall be delivered from persecution but through persecution. Neither is it that the followers of Christ will be delivered from pain and hardship while evil men will suffer. The emphasis of the gospel is that Christ will remain with his own in their anguish and bring lasting spiritual benefits through every bitter experience of life. On the other hand, evil men and imposters will steadily degenerate, becoming "worse and worse, deceiving and being deceived" (3:13). They practice deception so intensely that they come to believe it themselves. They are in that "bottomless pit" where men must ever be who are not on the solid foundation of fellowship with Christ. They have nothing to anticipate save deeper degradation and deeper anguish.

## IV. THE SCRIPTURAL FOUNDATIONS OF TRUE FAITH (3:14–17)

Timothy is encouraged in this passage to cling to the truth which had been forged into a personal conviction through his own experience. His conviction has been further deepened by his confidence in those who have taught him the ways of Christ. He has "learned" and "been assured" (3:14). In these two verbs Paul uses what is known as the aorist tense, which denotes completed action at some past time. "Timothy," says Paul, "has learned at a fixed time in the past finally and forever the essential truth of the Christian gospel." He must never deviate from it but must realize that, as the revelation of God, it must never be distorted but passed on intact even as he had received it.

### 1. *Steadfast Adherence to the Factual Side of Faith*

In the holy Scriptures, Timothy had been nurtured from his earliest infancy by his grandmother Lois and his mother Eunice. He had been taught the factual side of the revelation of God, which is prerequisite to the full salvation which comes through faith in Christ Jesus. It is the function of the Scriptures to introduce men to the Saviour. Timothy's training had not been in mythical traditions and secular writings but in the sacred writings of the Old Testament. Dr. Moffatt's translation is most meaningful: "Remember how you have known from childhood the sacred writings that can impart saving wisdom by faith in Christ Jesus" (3:15).

Our churches today do well to make great use of Bible study in their training programs and in all the teaching ministry. Paul's words to the Ephesian elders (Acts 20:32

ASV) are most significant: "I commend you to God, and to the word of his grace, which is able to build you up, and to give you the inheritance among all them that are sanctified."

## 2. *The Immutable Standard*

In contrast with the teachings of imposters, the Christian faith rests securely on its inspired Scriptures, which have been carefully preserved from generation to generation. Therefore, Paul calls Timothy to remember that "all scripture is given by inspiration of God," or is "God-breathed" (3:16). The Scriptures are the result of God's personal intervention on the plane of human history and of his personal encounter through the Spirit with his people and his prophets.

"Revelation" means God's presence in the events of history. "Inspiration" means his presence in the recording of those events. Just as God has been personally present in all of his redeeming activity in history and in the recording of the story of this activity, even so he is now present through his Holy Spirit to give spiritual discernment and comprehension to those who come to the holy Scriptures with sincere seeking hearts. The Word of God thus becomes the living word, piercing like a two-edged sword or like a surgeon's scalpel into the deepest recesses of the soul, prompting us to discern the direction which God is taking and prodding us to move with him (Heb. 4:12).

The unchangeable standard is in the Scriptures. Its immediate application to our contemporary needs is in the Holy Spirit. The Scriptures are the touchstone by which we may measure our interpretation of the guidance of the Holy Spirit. God never contradicts himself, and we may well be assured that he will never guide any man to go contrary to the clearly revealed principles of God as we have them in the Book of God.

The Scriptures are, therefore, "profitable" (3:16). As opposed to the unedifying contents of the heretical writings, which merely appeal to the intellect, the Scriptures have proved their serviceableness to humanity by supplying man's moral and spiritual needs for many centuries. Through gauging all false teachings by the Scriptures, Christian leaders may authoritatively reprove or refute all false doctrines.

The Scriptures are also profitable for correction or for "the raising up of them that fall." The strongest immediate instrument for restoring those who have departed from the truth is the Holy Bible. It is also the instrument for training men in the ways of right living.

> Holy Bible, Book divine,
> Precious treasure, thou art mine:
> Mine to tell me whence I came;
> Mine to teach me what I am.
>
> Mine to chide me when I rove,
> Mine to show a Saviour's love;
> Mine thou art to guide and guard;
> Mine to punish or reward.
>
> Mine to comfort in distress,
> Suffering in this wilderness;
> Mine to show, by living faith,
> Man can triumph over death.
>                                    JOHN BURTON, SR.

In the thought of Paul, the term, "man of God," has a primary reference to the minister of the gospel, although the principles stated apply to all in places of Christian leadership. The theme of this passage (3 : 14–17) is the moral equipment of the man of God. Paul views the man of God as being completely equipped for his work by the Scriptures. "No other book is essential," says Paul. "The Scriptures are completely adequate for every good work."

To share in the inspiration of the living Word of God makes a servant of Christ adequate to do the task which our Lord comprehensively defined as his work by quoting Isaiah

6:1. This passage has been paraphrased as follows, and should serve as a constant reminder of the Christian's divine orders:

> The Lord has annointed me to bring good news to poor people, to proclaim release to captives and sight to the blind, to send the crushed on their way with their troubles left behind them and to announce that God's time for doing all this has arrived.[2]

## V. THE CHRISTIAN WORKER'S SOLEMN CHARGE (4:1-5)

Few passages in the holy Scriptures have so solemn and searching a tone as do these verses. The very sound of them lays a spell upon the soul, which causes us to acknowledge immediately that the authority of heaven is behind them. It is small wonder that this passage should be used in the ordination service of most ministers of the gospel. Timothy, as well as every man entering the ministry, must remember that he is under the constant observation of the One before whom he shall stand at last in the judgment.

### 1. *A Pastor Awaiting Judgment*

Paul felt that the veil between time and eternity for him was very thin and that at any moment his Lord might step through that veil to call all men to judgment. The faithful will compose Christ's kingdom, which is to be consummated at his appearing.

A part of this charge seems to have been taken from an early Christian creed which spoke of Christ, "who shall judge the living and the dead" (4:1 ASV). The divine intervention is constantly impending. Men of God, therefore, must fulfil their ministry under the searching eyes of him before whom all men now in their graves and all who are still alive will stand in judgment.

In the face of the impending judgment, the minister has one responsibility and that is to preach the word to every man around him who is soon to stand with him in judgment. The "word" is the gospel of God's saving grace in Christ. Moffatt translates it, "Keep at it in season and out of season" (4:2). That is to say, your task is so urgent that you must preach whether the circumstances are favorable or not. Many a minister has rationalized away his responsibility by saying, "It is not a favorable season," or, "I was not in the mood," or he has nonchalantly pushed aside his opportunity by mis-interpreting the words of our Lord and saying, "Oh well, I am under orders not to cast my pearls before swine." "Never-theless," Paul says, as Easton translates it, "be at your task whether men will listen or not." [3]

## 2. Rebuking Error

Timothy is to "reprove" those who are in error until they are convinced that they are wrong. He is to "rebuke." This word in the New Testament is used only in the sense of cen-suring. Timothy then must strike out courageously against evil and all error. He must also "exhort," or preach "with all longsuffering and doctrine" (4:2), that is, "with the utmost patience and the most painstaking instruction." As the man of God strikes out against sin, he will in turn be rebuked, criticized, and maligned. He must patiently stay under his load, remembering that the faithful preaching of the full gospel involves suffering.

## 3. No Popularity Promised

The Christian leader must not anticipate the luxury of a day when men will gladly listen. In truth, just as good men grow in grace, even so bad men degenerate, until their ears are deafened to the divine voice and their hearts are hardened into stone. Men often inquire whether the world is getting better or worse. Perhaps the answer is that we see both eth-ical development and moral decline in the same society.

Of this we may also be sure, if men seek to substitute their own rationalizing for the revealed truth of God they will grow more and more impatient with the proclamation of revealed truth. Furthermore, they will flock to prophets who are hirelings, who will scratch their "itching ears" by saying what they want to hear. In the end they reach a point where they are no longer able to discern the truth. They turn away from it and "turn aside unto fables [myths]" (4:4 ASV).

The men Paul is describing were like those religious vagabonds who wander from church to church and imagine that the only thing wrong with them is that they are not hearing the right kind of preaching or teaching. They vainly imagine that all of their moral and spiritual ills could be healed if they could find the right magician. They imagine that religious truth is something that will transform them by intriguing them. Thus they ceaselessly wander after such myths, refusing to hear the truth of God and to yield to its steady and stabilizing demands.

Despite the clamor of the multitudes for the man of God to prophesy "smooth things," every Timothy must always be "sober" (4:5 ASV), or steady, in contrast with those who are drunken on the heady froth of religious fantasy. He must suffer as a good soldier and be an evangelist, a herald of the glad tidings of God's grace, which with sublime dogmatism refuses to deviate from the only saving message: "Neither is there salvation in any other: for there is none other name under heaven given among men, whereby we must be saved" (Acts 4:12). Moffatt writes, "Discharge all your duties as a minister" (4:5). The man of God who stays by the stuff and sincerely seeks the salvation of those whom God has given him to love will have no time to wander after myths.

## SUGGESTIONS FOR STUDY AND DISCUSSION

1. List the prerequisites for Christian service which our Lord laid down for his servants. Consider these as a basis for a moment of silent, personal self-searching.

2. Discuss the proper manner of dealing with error when it is taught in Christian churches.
3. Discuss the importance of clinging to the scriptural foundations of our faith.
4. Read together the pastor's solemn charge in 2 Timothy 4:1–5. To what extent does it apply specifically to ministers? What principles does it state which apply to all Christian workers?

---

[1] E. F. Scott, *The Pastoral Epistles* (New York: Harper & Brothers, 1936). Used by permission.

[2] W. M. Macgregor, *The Making of a Preacher* (London: Student Christian Movement Press, Ltd., 1945), p. 70. Used by permission. Out of print.

[3] Burton Scott Easton, *The Pastoral Epistles* (New York: Charles Scribner's Sons, 1947), pp. 186-187. Used by permission.

# CHAPTER 10

I. THE CROWN ANTICIPATED (4:6–8)
  1. Release from Bondage
  2. The Winning Side
  3. The Coronation

II. PAUL'S IMMEDIATE NEEDS (4:9–18)
  1. Human Fellowship
  2. A Warm Cloak
  3. The Books

III. FINAL GREETINGS (4:19–22)

# 10

# *The Martyr's Crown*

## I. THE CROWN ANTICIPATED (4:6–8)

The great apostle sets his solemn appeal within the context of his own coronation. He says, as Moffatt succinctly puts it, "My time to go has come" (4:6).

### 1. *Release from Bondage*

Paul does not dwell on the morbid side of death. For him it is a departure, or literally a "release." The picture is that of a great ship taking leave of the harbor to move out into its native habitat, where the glad, free winds of God play. Paul could say with Robert Freeman:

> When I go down to the sea by ship,
> And Death unfurls her sail,
> Weep not for me, for there will be
> A living host on another coast
> To beckon and cry, "All hail!"[1]
>
> ROBERT FREEMAN

For Paul death would be release from literal bondage. He considered the manner of his death as a sacrifice, for he was to face the executioner's axe. Yet so near was Christ to Paul that someone has said that he was unable to discern between the flash of the executioner's axe and the sheen on the garments of Christ.

The word translated "to be offered" was used to describe the presentation of a drink offering to God. Paul's life was to be poured out as a libation to God that others might, through his steadfast loyalty, come to God through Christ. Suffering and death take on a new meaning when they can be offered up to God with the perfect assurance that through them God will build his kingdom.

Paul lived in the constant awareness that before each new dawn he might be summoned to face the executioner's axe. Yet his imprisonment epistles glow with such expressions as, "Rejoice . . . and again, I say Rejoice" (Phil. 4:4). The cynic says, "Suppose Paul did remain true to Christ to the very end, what did it get him—perils by land and sea, exile, loneliness, and finally execution?" Nevertheless, if we look more deeply and steadily we may see that it got him the greatest thing that even God can bestow, the grace to look full into the executioner's face and beyond it, and the ability to rejoice in the perfect assurance that neither death nor life could separate him from that deathless love of the Redeemer that had brought the peace of God to stand sentry before the gates of his soul.

## 2. *The Winning Side*

Paul was further stabilized by the assurance that he was on the winning side of the battle. He does not say, "I have fought a good fight," as we have the verse in the King James Version. He is not talking about the kind of battle he has been able to wage for Christ. There could be nothing of such boastful arrogance in the soul of Paul at so solemn a moment. He is rather saying, "I have fought the good fight" (4:7 ASV). "I have been on the side of Christ. I have not followed imposters, not heretics." Paul had taken the battle seriously and had fought with all of his resources. Yet he had always known that ultimately the battle was the Lord's.

He had finished the "course," or the race. Paul was thinking also of his ministry as a long race in which he had often been weary and tempted to forfeit the crown. Yet he pushed on until he crossed the goal.

"Finally," Paul says, "I have kept the faith." Many see this also as an athletic metaphor and translate it, "I have kept my pledge." Thus Paul viewed his total life in terms of the Greek games, which called for austere discipline and rugged endurance. He had fought like a pugilist, had endured like a distance runner, and had carefully kept his pledge to follow the rules.

### 3. *The Coronation*

In the fuller sense, Paul regards "the faith" as that deposit which Christ had given him and which he was now returning untarnished to the One who waits the coming of his own when the battle is over and the race is won. Nothing new remained but for Paul to enter into his coronation (4:8). The crown, which was the due reward of his righteousness, awaited him. The effectual grace of God had wrought true righteousness in the pattern of Paul's life, and now he was to receive the crown as the reward of his righteousness.

The Greco-Roman world of the first century took the crown as the symbol of immortality. Paul, then, was saying, "The righteous Judge will surely welcome me into the fellowship of life eternal with all whose lives are pledged to him and who long for his appearing, to establish his everlasting kingdom" (4:8).

## II. Paul's Immediate Needs (4:9–18)

Paul turned from his confident farewell to add a postscript in which he describes three needs.

### 1. *Human Fellowship*

First of all, Paul needed Timothy's companionship. The apostle was now a lonely and desolate prisoner. He therefore writes, "Do your best to come to me soon." Demas, Crescens, and Titus had all gone away. Demas, in contrast to those "who love his appearing," loved instead "this present world" and thus deserted Paul, perhaps to enter secular business in Thessalonica (4:10). Crescens departed, probably on church business in Gaul where, according to tradition, he was martyred under the Emperor Trajan. Titus departed to Dalmatia, in southern Illyricum on the eastern shore of the Adriatic Sea.

Luke, the beloved physician, remained steadfast and loyal. Twice in the New Testament Luke and Demas are mentioned as being together (Col. 4:14; Philemon 24). Luke's loyalty is all the more significant and magnified in that, after Demas yielded to the lure of the world, he alone was left to be an intrepid companion to Paul and to comfort his "thorn in the flesh," perhaps more by his presence than by his medication.

Yet for all Luke's loyalty, Paul still wanted the companionship of Timothy, his son in the ministry. He desired also that Timothy should bring Mark with him. Apparently Paul and Mark had been reconciled since their parting in Acts 14:36-41. The apostle now saw Mark as "useful . . . for ministering" (4:11 ASV). Perhaps Mark was to take the place of Tychicus, who was to take the place Timothy was vacating in Ephesus.

## 2. *A Warm Cloak*

Paul also wanted his cloak, which probably was a heavy wool garment, to protect him from the winter. It was getting cold in Rome. The cold, wintry winds would pass through the subterranean corridors of the Mamertine Prison, chilling the bones of the aged apostle to the very marrow. This was the only cloak Paul had. Those who seem to feel that the Christian gospel promises an abundance of material comforts to all followers of Christ need to remember that Paul was so poor that he could not afford to lose an old cloak at Troas. We know nothing about Carpus save that he was the custodian of the cloak of Paul.

### 3. *The Books*

Paul wanted his books, for he was a student to the very end and wished to feed his mind during his lonely hours. Especially did he desire the parchments (4:13). The books were the papyrus rolls. We can only speculate as to their nature. The parchments were very expensive writing materials. Some have contended that these had precious writings upon them, such as the Old Testament Scriptures. Others have felt that they were simply writing materials for Paul's letters.

Alexander, the coppersmith who did Paul much evil, cannot be positively identified, for Alexander was a most common name. Goodspeed thinks he was a metalworker who had strongly opposed the work of Paul. The apostle, therefore, saw him not merely as one inflicting wrong upon himself but as one opposing the cause of Christ. Timothy must, therefore, beware of him. "For he has been bitterly hostile to anything I have said" (4:15 Moffatt). Timothy must also know that vengeance belongs to the Lord. "The Lord will reward [requite] him according to his works" (4:14). Timothy, therefore, was not to concern himself with avenging the wrongs Alexander has done against the church. "Dearly beloved avenge not yourselves, but rather give place unto wrath: for it is written, Vengeance is mine; I will repay, saith the Lord" (Rom. 12:19).

Paul still remembered with sadness that, during the preliminary investigation of his case, the Christians in Rome were so devoid of courage that every one of them forsook him. "At my first defence no one took my part" (4:16 ASV). Paul considered it such a major sin to desert a man of God in his hour of need that he prayed that God might not charge this action against his fellow Christians. Paul is not being sentimental and saying that such treason was a minor matter. Rather is he saying that it was such a major matter that he must pray that God would bestow mercy upon such deserters.

Although Paul was abandoned by Christian men, yet the Lord did not abandon him. The divine companionship steadied Paul to the very end, giving him adequate strength in his most perilous hours "to make a full statement of the Gospel" (4:17 Moffatt). His personal defense was so adequate that he was delivered thereby out of the "lion's mouth." This means he was spared from death. The "lion's mouth" was an expression often used to describe extreme danger (Psalms 22:21; 7:2). Through Paul's peril he was enabled to fulfil his highest ambition, which was to preach to the Grand Assembly in Rome.

Paul was assured that no attack upon him could do him permanent harm, for God would stand by him and ultimately bring his servant "unto his heavenly kingdom" (4:18). This thought lifted Paul's soul and sent it soaring on the wings of this doxology: "To whom be glory for ever and ever. Amen."

## III. FINAL GREETINGS (4:19–22)

How could Paul ever forget Prisca (Priscilla) and Aquila! He had lived with them for more than a year and a half in Corinth. He delighted to think often of them. In contrast with his fickle companions, they had risked their necks for his life (Rom. 16:14). Paul also salutes the household of Onesiphorus who had "oft refreshed" him (2 Tim. 1:16).

How diversified were the gifts of Paul's followers! Erastus (Rom. 16:23) was the city treasurer of Corinth. Trophimus was an Ephesian who met Paul at Troas, journeyed with him to Jerusalem, and innocently became the occasion of Paul's arrest. Now he was ill and the apostle had not forgotten him. Not even tradition gives us any light on the identity of Eubulus. Pudens, according to tradition, was a Roman senator who was one of Peter's converts. Linus, according to Eusebius, was bishop of Rome for twelve years after Peter and Paul had met their martyrdom. Claudia was, according to tradition, the mother of Linus. These personalities give us some insight into the universality of the Christian gospel in its appeal to all classes and conditions of men.

This epistle closes on a note of urgency. "Do thy diligence to come before winter" (4:21). Why before winter? Not only because Paul was in desperate need of companionship, his cloak, and his books, but also because he had a premonition that he would not last through the winter. "The time of my departure is at hand" (4:6). He knew that if Timothy did not come before winter, he would never see him on earth again. It was before winter or never.

The late Dr. Clarence E. Macartney had a great sermon entitled "Come Before Winter" which he preached annually in his pulpit.[2] In it he emphasized that the sailing season in the Mediterranean closed with the coming of winter and no ships would sail until April. Therefore, he delighted to imagine that Timothy, immediately upon receiving the letter from Paul, departed for Troas, picked up the books and parchments, went by the house of Carpus, got the cloak, sailed to Neapolis, climbed the Ignatian way, crossed the plains of Philippi through Macedonia, took another ship to Brundisium, and traveled up the Appian Way to Rome. Then he made his way out to the prison, found Paul, read to him from the Old Testament, wrote his last letters, and finally walked with him to the place of execution by the pyramids of Cestius and saw him receive the crown of glory.

Paul concludes this letter with a brief prayer which is rich beyond all our comprehension. "The Lord Jesus Christ be with thy spirit" (4:22) is a petition that the same Lord Jesus, whose vital indwelling in Paul had made him adequate for all of life's demands and duties, would ever be with Timothy. "Grace be with you" is a petition that the overflowing mercy of God, which no man can merit and which is greater than all our sins and all our needs, may be the portion of every man of God.

## SUGGESTIONS FOR STUDY AND DISCUSSION

1. Discuss Paul's attitude toward death as depicted in the metaphors "departure," "fought the good fight," "finished the race," "kept the faith," "crown of righteousness."
2. Discuss the pathos of Paul's final days on earth as reflected in his imprisonment, proverty, and loneliness.
3. Let members of the class mention what they think stabilized Paul in his final hours. List their suggestions on the blackboard.

---

[1] Robert Freeman "Beyond the Horizon," *The Funeral Encyclopedia* by Charles L. Wallis (New York: Harper & Brothers, 1953), p. 214. Reprinted by permission of Harper & Brothers.
[2] Clarence E. Macartney, *Come Before Winter* (Nashville: Abingdon Press, 1945), p. 9. Used by permission.

# Questions for Review and Examination

## CHAPTER 1

1. Why did Paul call Timothy "my own son in the faith" (1 Tim. 1:2)?
2. Summarize the relation of a Christian to the law as stated in 1 Timothy 1:8–11.
3. Tell of Timothy's appointment as Paul's successor in 1 Timothy 1:18–20.

## CHAPTER 2

4. Why should Christians pray for pagan rulers?
5. What did Paul mean when he insisted that Christ "gave himself a ransom for all"?
6. Why were women refused conspicuous places in the life of the church in Paul's day?

## CHAPTER 3

7. What did Paul mean when he insisted that the man who would be a pastor must be "blameless"?
8. Discuss the pastor's care of his children.
9. Mention the rewards which come to a faithful deacon.

## CHAPTER 4

10. Discuss the necessity for strong discipline and rigid training in the ministry.
11. How is a young minister or other Christian leader to overcome the handicap of his youth?
12. What did Paul mean when he urged Timothy to "meditate upon these things" (1 Tim. 4:15)?

## CHAPTER 5

13. What did Paul mean by "widows indeed" in 1 Timothy 5:3?
14. What did Paul mean by "double honor" in 1 Timothy 5:17?
15. Summarize what is said in 1 Timothy 6:2–5 about the necessity for sound teaching.

## Chapter 6

16. What is said about the Christian's warfare in 1 Timothy 6: 11–16?
17. How did Paul say Christians may treasure up for themselves a good foundation?
18. What was Paul's supreme concern for Timothy?

## Chapter 7

19. What did Paul mean when he urged Timothy to "stir up the gift of God" (2 Tim. 1:6)?
20. What did Paul mean when he said Jesus Christ brought life and immortality to light (2 Tim. 1:10)?
21. Show how the gospel was spread through personal friendships (2 Tim. 1:15–18).

## Chapter 8

22. Discuss the pastor as a good soldier.
23. Discuss the death that brings life (2 Tim. 2:8–13).
24. What did Paul mean by "rightly dividing the word of truth" (2 Tim. 2:15)?

## Chapter 9

25. Discuss the proper attitude for a Christian leader to take toward controversy.
26. What was the original meaning of the word "meek"?
27. Discuss Paul's example in dealing with false teachers.

## Chapter 10

28. What did Paul mean when he said, "I have fought the good fight" (2 Tim. 4:7)?
29. Name the things which Paul desired most for Timothy to bring to him.
30. What did Paul mean when he wrote "Do thy diligence to come before winter" (2 Tim. 4:21)?

# Date Due

| 9/20/78 | | | |
|---|---|---|---|
| | | | |
| 12/12/78 | | | |
| 4/22/85 | | | |
| | | | |
| | | | |
| | | | |
| | | | |
| | | | |
| | | | |
| | | | |
| | | | |
| | | | |
| | | | |
| | | | |
| | | | |
| | | | |
| | | | |
| | | | |

Code 4386-04, CLS-4, Broadman Supplies, Nashville, Tenn., Printed in U.S.A.